THE EOLIAN ISLANDS: PEARLS OF THE MEDITERRANEAN

The Editor took on the work of composing this guide with a sentimental approach. The Islands have been described by all those writing with love for the land in which they were born or have chosen to live. Many thanks to Franco Italiano, Tilde Paino, Nino Paino, Umberto Spigo, Giuseppe Lo Cascio, Luigi Amato, Giuseppe Iacolino, Riccardo Gullo, Marcello Saija, Amelia Ruggeri, Antonio Brundu, Kurt Wahlen, Mauro Coltelli, Luigi Barrica, Gisella and Aldo Ardizzone.
We would like to give special thanks to the photographers who have illustrated the guide with images that do justice to the beauty of these islands.
We have taken advice from Bernard Michaud for Alcudi, Aldo Ardizzone for Filicudi, Antonio Brundu, Mauro Leva, Vincenzo Mirenda and Patrizia Lopez for Salina, Marco Spisso for Vulcano, Rosa Maria Longo and Roraima De Francesco for Stromboli, Susanna Tesoriero and Carola Tesoriero for Panarea, Gianfranco Girone, Rosario Mangano for Lipari.
Thanks to all those, not wishing to forget anyone, who have helped to re-read, correct and improve this publication.
Finally, thanks to the tireless Salvo Campo.

The Editor dedicates this guide
to his daughter Federica.

PHOTOGRAPHS AND ILLUSTRATIONS

Riccardo Lombardo: *page1,4,6,7,13,14,16,17,18,19,20,22,23,24,28,29,32,34,36,38,40,41,42,45,46,47,48,49,53,54,55,56,57,60, 61,64,65,68,69,70,71, 75,77,79,81,83,84,85,86,89,90,94,96,100,106,112,113,114,115,118,119,120,121,124,126,128,129,130,134, 135,136,137,140,141.*
Salvo Campo: *page 3,12,15,28,29,30,31,32,34,36,37,39,51,52,57,60, 62,65,68,69,72,73,74,86,87,90,91,105,108,119,127,129.*
Lou Embo Roiter: *page 5,10,28,29,38,43,44,62,70,82,101,103,111,112,113,117,119,121.*
Roberto Rinaldi: *page 18,19,22,23,86,88,98,99,101,104,105,106,110,118.*
Giulio Veggi: *page 22,84,105,119,140.*
Antonio Brundu: *page 78,80,83,92,93.*
Filippo Massari: *page 59,139.*
T Licciardiello: *page 59,138.*
Angelo Panzera: *page 17,20,131,132.*
Aldo Ardizzone: *page 131.*
Giuseppe Lo Cascio: *page 50,52.*
Franco Italiano: *page 25,97.*
Calleo: *page 28,29,74,84.*
Giuffrè: *page 75.*
Mauro Coltelli: *page 116,117.*
Amelia Ruggeri: *page 81.*
Cover photo: 1ST AND 4TH PAGE, LOMBARDO; 2ND PAGE CAMPO; 3RD PAGE LICCIARDELLO

TRANSLATIONS

FRENCH: **Bernard Michaud**
ENGLISH: **Nicholas Whithorn**
GERMAN: **Doreen Lamek**

MAPS: **Edizioni Turistiche Ippolito** - Messina
From the official documentation of the Hydrographic Institute of the Navy, authorization to reproduce N° 2 of 20. 3. 1997.
From the printing works of the Comune di Lipari: authorization N° Prot. 42211 of 15. 1. 1997.
From the printing works of the Geographical Military Institute: authorization N° 4535 of 14. 1. 1997
According to Law 02. 02. 1960 No 68, Nulla osta for distribution N° 137 of 16/4/1997
Translations and editing with desktop publishing

EDITORIAL CONSULTANT: **Margaret Donaldson**

EDITORIAL CO-ORDINATION: **Tiziana Leva**

WELCOME TO THE EOLIAN ISLANDS

The Eolian islands get their name from Aeolus, lord of the winds, who according to Homer had his kingdom here. They are islands full of surprises and contrasts. When you draw near to them, by ferry or hydrofoil, you can't help being overwhelmed by the magnificence of the scenery and tempted to explore.

"Wandering islands", over thousands of years eruptions have often modified their size and appearance. The coasts and depths are amazing, but the interior is also full of charm; imposing volcanoes, still active, strange rock formations, thick vegetation on Salina, archaeological treasures and prehistoric villages on Lipari, Panarea and Filicudi and the artefacts given up by the sea and jealously guarded in the Archaeological Museum of Lipari.

Islands of wind and sun which have forged the character and identity of the islanders.

Despite the ups and downs of history and the changes imposed by the modern world, this identity has survived, along with its customs and traditions.

The Eolian islanders are kind, friendly people who will welcome you with warmth.

Let's go then, from one island to another, following an ancient route around the clear waters of this legendary sea.

We were looking for a place to live a quiet life, far away from chaos, loud sirens, from traffic queues and aggression at the traffic lights, from vicious people.
We were looking for a place where we could smile about our future instead of being afraid, without having to fight over a parking space: a place where our home continued beyond the gate.
We were looking for the sea, sun, scent, silence. All this to continue being ourselves. So we left for distant places. We saw, tried and in the end our exoticism was fulfilled. Just round the corner, in the Aeolian archipelago.
We live here and we want to offer the possibility of experiencing this atmosphere to whoever has the same desires as us.

GISELLA AND ALDO ARDIZZONE

Few words are necessary to convey the strong attraction of the islands. In the past, like today, great and famous travellers like Dumas, Houel, Guy de Maupassant, De Dolomieu and the Archduke Luigi Salvatore of Austria, explored places and studied the economy, traditions and customs giving them early recognition in important works like the eight volumes of the Archduke of Austria.
The Aeolian islands are volcanic creatures born from the active presence of the four elements: air, water, earth and fire. They emerged from the sea during the pleistocene period and since then have changed shape several times. Evolution is still ongoing and indeed, in 1955, near Stromboli, a small new island emerged, then sank again; on Lipari, the pumice and obsidian flows of Mount Pelato and Forgia Vecchia date back to 729 AD, the volcanoes on Vulcano, Lipari and Panarea, water and mud baths remind us that all is not dormant.
The islands offer their natural beauty to tourists, scholars and sea lovers. A clean sea, still full of fish, grottoes and high cliffs, crags and fine, black sand beaches, sulphur springs and white pumice mountains and all the charm of an island environment.
You can get there all year round by hydrofoil and ferry and easy connections are one of the reasons for the increase in tourism. You can board from Naples by car without having to go to Sicily. In summer, hydrofoils serve the islands, with varying daily routes, to Reggio Calabria, Gioia Tauro, Messina, Palermo, Cefalù, Sant'Agata di Militello, Giardini and Milazzo. And, furthermore, a small airport on Lipari is being planned.
The climate is mild and in winter the thermometer never drops below 10°. Summers are not torrid as they are lightened by a sea breeze. That is why, even out of season, long, pleasant stays are possible. In spring, the vegetation that carpets the islands is an explosion of colour and scent. Once they were covered by thick woods, but, today, the Mediterranean scrub prevails. Man has cleared almost every available centimetre of woodland to cultivate grapes, olives, capers, pulses and vegetables. The widespread terraces, now abandoned, are proof of great human work over thousands of years.
Man and geographical features have given a different stamp to each island.
Filicudi and Alicudi are "antistress refuges" with an uncontaminated environment.
Panarea is a fashionable island, the destination of elite tourists.
Stromboli and Vulcano, rough and wild, attract young, rather bohemian tourists.
Salina, the greenest, with its twin mountains, is chosen by families with children because of its peace and quiet.
Lipari, the biggest and most heavily populated, the municipality which administers all the other islands (excluding Salina), offers comfort, space, all kinds of services, including a fully-equipped hospital and a sheltered port.

Page on the left: Porticello's Beach (Lipari)
Photo on the right: Madonna della Catena's Sanctuary - Quattropani (Lipari)
Following page: Acquacalda

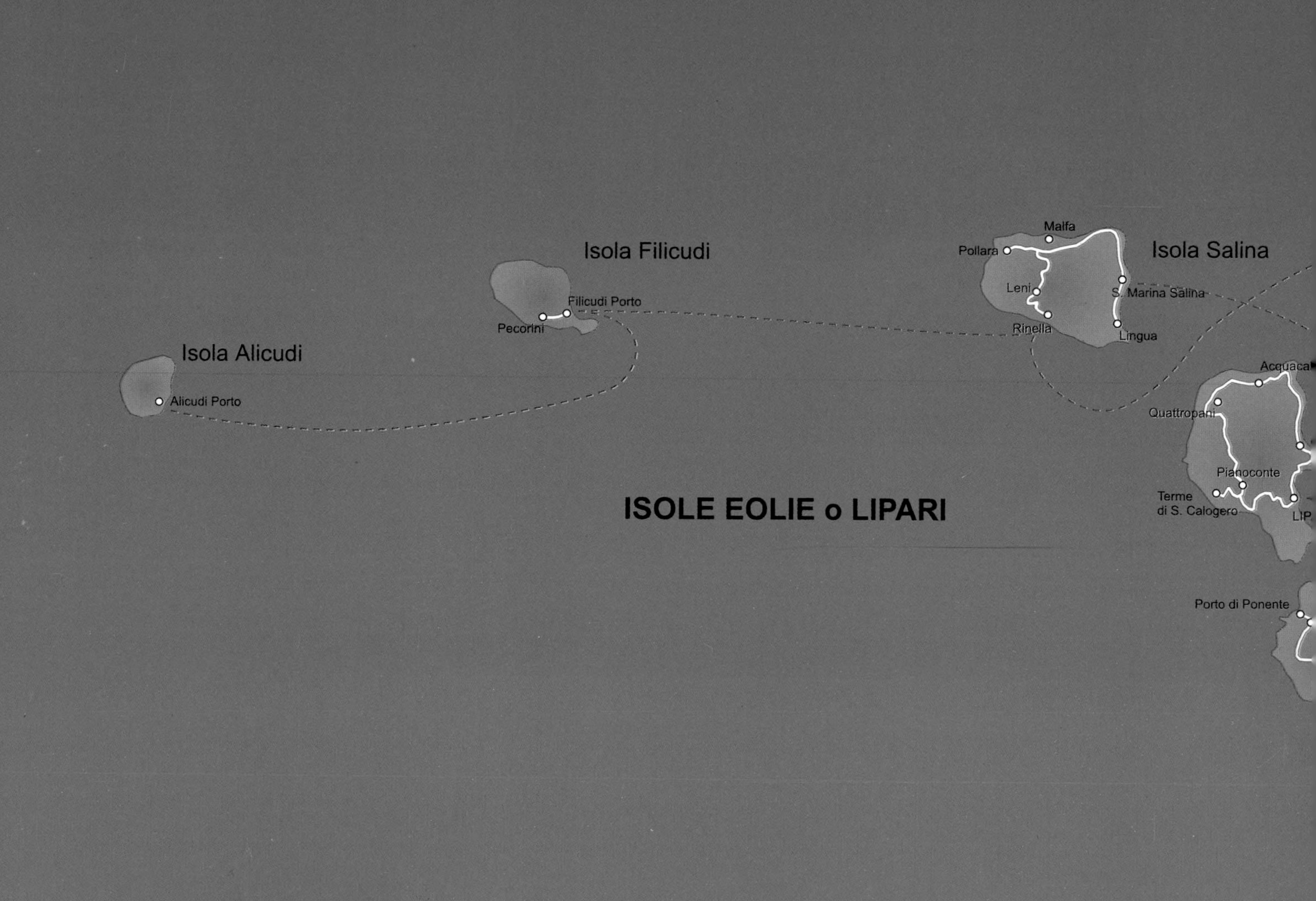
Isola Filicudi
Filicudi Porto
Pecorini
Isola Alicudi
Alicudi Porto
Malfa
Pollara
Isola Salina
Leni
S. Marina Salina
Rinella
Lingua
Acquacalda
Quattropani
Pianoconte
Terme
di S. Calogero
ISOLE EOLIE o LIPARI
Porto di Ponente
C. Cala
Gioiosa Marea
Galbato
C. d'Orlando
Scoglio di Brolo
Piraino
Brolo
Capo d'Orlando
S. Gregorio
Gliaca
S. Costantino
S. Lucia Marina
Forno Marina
Lacco
Salinà
Montagnare
Matini

Isola Strombolicchio
S. Bartolo
S. Vincenzo
Ginostra
Isola Stromboli
Isola Basiluzzo
Isola Panarea
S. Pietro
Lipari
Levante
Isola Vulcano
Gelso
C. Rasocolmo
Spartà
Acqualadroni
S. Saba
Casa Bianca
C. Peloro
Massa S. Giorgio
M. S. Nicolò
M. S. Lucia
Mortelle
Rodia
Castanea
d. Furie
M. S. Giovanni
Faro Sup.
Ganzirri
Orto Liuzzo
Curcuraci
Salice
S. Agata
Cannitello
Golfo di Milazzo
C. Milazzo
P.ta Messinese
Baronia
Paradiso
Croce al Promontorio
P.ta del Tono
Tono
Milazzo
Riviera di Ponente
Riviera di Levante
Villafranca Tirrena
Rometta Marea
Fondaconuovo
Spadafora
Venetico Marina
Fondachello
Scala
Monforte Marina
Giammoro
Archi
Gesso
Urni
P.lla
Castanea
Pace
Contemplazione
Bauso
S. Nicola
Rizzotti
Paradiso
Villa
S. Giovanni
Calvaruso
Serro
P.lla
S. Rizzo
Annunziata
Cavaliere
Maiorani
Cavallari
S. Andrea
Rapano
Badiazza
MESSINA
Catarratti
Camaro
Saponara
Tracoccia
Valdina
Roccavaldina
S. Giovanni
Fossazzo
S. Pietro
S.ta Maria
d. Grazie
S.ta Marina
Bastione
Olivarella
Corriolo
Cattafi
Pace
del Mela
Torregrotta
Zifronte
Condrò
Carda
S. Salvatore
S. Pietro
Rometta
S. Cono
S.ta Domenica
Nunziatella
Bordonaro
Cumia
Santo
S. Filippo Sup.
S. Lucia
Gazzi
Contesse
Pistunina
S. Filippo Inf.
Zafferia
Larderia Sup.
Tipoldo
Inf.
Mili S. Marco
Mili S. Pietro
Galati Sup.
Mili Marina
Moleti
Tremestieri
Galati Marina
S. Stefano Medio
S. Stefano Briga
S. Margherita
Stretto di Messina
Campo Calabro
Catona
Gallico Marina
Archi
Golfo di Patti
Calderà
Meri
S. Filippo del Mela
Soccorso
S. Pier Niceto
Monforte S. Giorgio
Pellegrino
Barcellona Pozzo di G.
S.ta Lucia del Mela
Cannistrà
S. Paolo
Lido Marchesana
Castroreale Terme
Marchesana Marina
Tonnarella
C. Tindari
Marina di Patti
Mongiove
Santuario
Patti
Moreri
Scala
Oliveri
Falcone
Terme
Portosalvo
S. Biagio
Nasari
La Gala
Proto-notaro
Migliardo

LIPARI: FROM THE PREHISTORIC TO THE GRAECO-ROMAN AGE

Since 1928 Lipari has been a centre of archaeological research. The discovery of the necropolis in Contrada Diana was due to senator Orsi and since 1946, the commitment and activity of the experienced archaeologists Luigi Bernabò Brea and Madeleine Cavalier has allowed the discovery of all the other archaeological sites. The abundance of finds testifies to the importance, since 5000 BC, of the Aeolian archipelago that acted as a centre of exchange between East and West.

Obsidian certainly represented, even since before the Bronze Age, a source of wealth. This sharp, black, volcanic glass, widely used in the making of arms, tools and utensils, was exported all over the Mediterranean. It was probably obsidian that awakened the interests of the first people originating from Sicily, who settled on the high plains of Lipari at Castellaro Vecchio and on Salina at Rinicedda.

In the Castello area and at its base, the wind blowing over the high plains, deposited, century after century, volcanic ash which covered and preserved traces of every age that succeeded it. This stratigraphy is unique in its kind.

It is believed that the first inhabitants, devoted to agriculture, were replaced by others from the Dalmatian coast. The latter settled on the castle rock and gave a new boost to the economy and to the island culture, as painted and decorated ceramic remains testify. With the passing of centuries, the community grew and moved from the castle rock to Contrada Diana. On Lipari and the smaller islands they established small agricultural settlements and a merchant fleet (3000 BC).

New cultures followed: the one called Pianoconte (2700), which spread over the Lipari plateau and the smaller islands, and that of Piano Quartara (second half of the 3rd millenium BC) marked a period of recession.

However, the settlements in the last centuries in the 3rd millenium BC testify the new prosperity.

On all the islands, the Capo Graziano culture was affirmed, of which the most famous discoveries were made on Filicudi. These relate to the remains of two villages. The first near the shore, the second on the top of a hill. From this, it can be deduced that the population, perhaps fearing raids

Prehistoric village at Punta Milazzese - Panarea

THE EOLIAN ISLANDS FROM PREHISTORIC TIMES TO THE ARABS

MIDDLE NEOLITHIC

The final centuries of the 5th millennium BC: first phase of the Eolian neolithic. Cultural facies of Castellaro Vecchio.

First centuries of the fourth millennium BC: second phase of the Eolian neolithic. Period of three-coloured pottery. Castle Rock of Lipari inhabited.

Around the middle of the fourth millennium: third phase of the Eolian neolithic. Period of intricate spiral design pottery.

Second half of the 4th and early 3rd millennium BC: culture of Diana.

ENEOLITHIC

First phase of the eneolithic

First half of the 3rd millennium BC: cultural facies of Diana-Spatarella.

Middle eneolithic

Around the middle of the 3rd millennium BC: culture of Piano conte (which begins to show, however, before the middle of the millennium, probably around 2700-2600 BC).

Upper eneolithic

Second half of the 3rd millennium BC: culture of Piano Quartara.

BRONZE AGE

Early Bronze Age

Last centuries of the 3rd millennium BC - 1430 BC: culture of Capo Graziano.

Middle Bronze Age

*c.*1430-1270 BC: Milazzese culture.

Late Bronze Age

*c.*1270-1125 BC: Ausonio I.

Late 12th - late 10th or early 9th century BC: Ausonio II.

Late 10th, early 9th century - *c.*580 BC: the Eolian archipelago is completely uninhabited, with the exception of Lipari, where, according to Diodoro Siculo, on the arrival of the Greeks a very small number of natives lived.

GREEK AGE

580-576 BC: Groups of inhabitants of Cnido and Rhodes, survivors of the unsuccessful expedition of Pentathlos in western Sicily, land at Lipari, under the leadership of Gorgo, Testore and Epiterside and found the colony of Lipari.

6th century - 474 BC: Naval conflicts with the Etruscans and numerous victories judging by the donations to the Sanctuary of Apollo at Delphi. Probably in the third decade of the 5th century BC Lipàra was briefly conquered by the Etruscans, who sacrificed Theodotos, one of the most strenuous defenders of Apollo.

474 BC: The Etruscan threat to Lipari ends with their defeat at Cuma at the hands of Ierone of Siracusa. During the 5th century stable dwellings, of an agricultural nature, are set up on other islands.

427-426 BC: As an ally of Siracusa against Athens in the Peloponnesian war, Lipari suffers Athenian raids (and from allies of Athens).

397-396 BC: During the war between Carthage and Siracusa, Lipàra is conquered by the Carthaginian fleet, under the command of Imilcone, which imposes on the town a ransom of 30 talents.

393 BC: The arconte (supreme magistrate) of Lipàra, Timasiteo, returns to Rome the gold crater (a tenth of a Veio's length) that a Roman ship, boarded by Liparese pirates, was taking to the sanctuary of Delphi in Greece.

389 BC: During the conflict between Dionigi of Siracusa and the Italiots, Tearide, Dionigi's brother, captures ten enemy ships from the Reggio fleet in the waters of Lipari.

304 BC: Lipàra is attacked treacherously by Agatocle, tyrant of Siracusa, who imposes a ransom of 50 talents; the ships of Siracusa that carry back the booty (votive offerings to Aeolus and Efesto from the prytaneum of the town) are sunk in a storm, seen as a sign of divine anger.

264 BC: During the first Punic war Lipari allies with Carthage against Rome and becomes the operating base of the Carthaginian admiral Hannibal.

260-257 BC: The waters of Lipari are the scene of important episodes in the war between Carthaginians and Romans, who try unsuccessfully to conquer the island on two occasions.

252-251 BC: Lipari is destroyed and conquered by the Romans under the command of the consul Aurelio Cotta.

ROMAN AGE

218 BC: During the second Punic war nine Carthaginian triremes take refuge at Lipari.

First half of the 2nd century BC: formation of Vulcanello.

69 BC: Lipari, civitas decumana (with the obligation to pay the "decima"), along with many other Sicilian towns, suffers the outrage of Verre, pro-praetor of Sicily, referred to by Cicero in one of his works.

37 BC: Octavius, during the civil war with Sesto Pompeo, son of Cneo Pompeo, deports the inhabitants of Lipari to Dicearchia in Campania because they support the latter. Shortly afterwards Sesto Pompeo places strategic bases in the Eolian islands, especially on Lipari.

36 BC: The fleet of Octavius, commanded by Agrippa, obtains an important victory, between Lipari and Milazzo, over Sesto Pompeo, who will later that year be finally defeated in the naval battle of Nauloco, near Capo Peloro.

Pliny the Elder (AD 23-79), in the 3rd book of his "Naturalis Historia," mentions Lipari as "oppidum civium romanorum," that is a "Roman town" whose inhabitants had Roman citizenship and enjoyed administrative autonomy.

AD 205: Plantilla, wife of the Emperor Caracalla, is interned on Lipari with her brother Plauziano.

AD 417: Attalo Prisco, already nominated Emperor of Alarico, is interned on Lipari with the Emperor Onorio.

BYZANTINE AGE

AD 506-511: Teodorico interns the curial Rovino, accused of murder, on Vulcano.

AD 543: The Goths, after their conquest of Naples, establish a naval base on Lipari.

By the 6th century AD the remains of San Bartolomeo are kept in Lipari (according to San Gregorio of Tours).

First half of the 8th century AD: Eruption of Monte Pelato.

AD 838: Lipari is sacked and destroyed by the Arabs. The remains of San Bartolomeo are transferred to Benevento.

Taken from "Archeologia viva" n. 46
Edizioni Giunti

The dating of the phases of Eolian prehistory is the work of Luigi Bernabò Brea and Madeleine Cavalier.

and invasions, was forced to move to a place which was more easily defended. This also happened on Lipari, where the population moved from the base of the castle rock to the summit.
It is believed that they were people originating from Greece, perhaps the "Eoli", whom Homer spoke about in the Odyssey, who were attracted by the strategic position which allowed control over the straits of Messina and trade routes with the East, and gave life to this phase which lasted more than seven centuries.
Towards the 15th century BC Lipari was conquered by Sicilian people who started the "Milazzese culture" named after the promontory on Panarea. Invasions followed and a new population from the Italic peninsula appeared (1270-1125 BC circa).
The "Ausoni" king Liparo gave the current name to the biggest island. This new culture superimposed the castle rock constructions and this phase, called Ausonio I, perhaps refers to the discovery of an urn containing 80 kg of bronze ingots, various arms and utensils.
Ausonio I was succeeded by Ausonio II towards the end of the 12th century BC, with evident signs of destruction.
A period of great prosperity followed, which lasted 150 years and during this time commercial exchange with Sardinia and Greece flourished, as the great quantity of ceramics discovered testifies.
In 850 BC the Lipari fortress was stormed and the whole archipelago remained uninhabited for 3 centuries. The descendants of the survivors of the terrible destruction (only 500 according to Diodoro) welcomed to a great degree towards 580 BC, the Cnidi, a group of Greek colonisers who fought against Etruscan pirates winning splendid naval victories. Colonisers and natives fused together to form one population which gave it an equal social organisation. While a number of the inhabitants dedicated themselves to agriculture and rearing sheep, others saw to defence and the construction of ships. Lipari was rebuilt in Greek style: the acropolis on the rock and the village at the base of its walls. The new community progressed and the construction of a fleet allowed them to acquire a pre-eminent position in the lower Tyrrhenian Sea.
This happy period has been proved by archaeological discoveries: the walls and ruins of a tower; the necropolis of Contrada Diana, with numerous tombs and relative funeral decorations, so far intact; the excavated shrine, 7 metres deep and formed like a cistern, with ritually broken offerings. Through the ceramic fragments it has been possible to reconstruct many urns, exhibited at the museum, which testify to the high standard reached by manufacturing artisans.
For a long time, Lipari was allied to the people of Syracuse in order to confront the expansionist attempts of the Carthaginians and Athenians.
The 4th century BC represents the peak of economic prosperity with a town of vast proportions and the production of ceramics painted in many colours and terracotta decorated with theatrical scenes.
In 304 BC Lipari was sacked by the Syracusans of Agatocle and its decline began. During the first Punic War, it was allied with the Carthaginians against the Romans. After alternate fortunes, the Carthaginian fleet was destroyed by Caio Duilio and Lipari, besieged, was devastated in 251 BC marking the beginning of Roman domination.

Umberto Spigo

Archaeological digs at Lipari Castle

The prosperity that Lipari enjoyed during the two centuries of Greek rule came to an end with the Roman conquest. The island, small but independent, had reached a level of wealth, which is shown by the production of refined pottery and an unusually large town.
After the destruction, massacres and deportations of the Roman conquest a long period of poverty followed. Lipari became a provincial town of no importance, subject to the Castle garrison.
It became a municipium in the imperial age, a place of deportations and internment.
From the third century onwards, under Byzantine influence, it was possibly a bishopric and the destination of hermits in search of refuge. The Christian community recognised San Bartolomeo as its patron and his remains became an object of worship.
Digs which brought to light the remains of an arena, spas and roads show that Lipari had regained its vitality by the 5th century. In 543 the Goths established a naval base on Lipari.
In the early Middle Ages Lipari declined rapidly, both as a result of volcanic activity on Monte Pelato and Forgia Vecchia in 729, and because of continuing raids by the Arabs who devastated the town and deported its inhabitants in 838.
The islands were uninhabited for two centuries until the arrival of the Normans in 1083 and the foundation of a monastery by Benedictine monks. In 1091 the monastery obtained the feudal seignory over the Eolian islands, with a bull of Pope Urban II. The abbot of the monastery, Brother Ambrogio, promulgated in 1095 the "Constitutum," which granted to citizens and their heirs property of the land they cared for. In order to colonise Lipari the right to property was extended to outsiders, but only after having cultivated the land for three years and with the obligation to hand it back to local people in the event of selling it. A concrete policy of repopulating the islands was started up through the exploitation of land abandoned after the Saracen incursion of 838. A photographic reproduction of the document can be seen in Room XXVI of the Museum of Lipari. The cathedral dedicated to San Bartolomeo was built next to the Benedictine Abbey, a century after the arrival of the Normans, with material taken from the Greek walls, on the ruins of the proto-Christian one, which had in turn perhaps replaced a Graeco-Roman temple. The magnificence of the Cathedral demonstrates that the town had come back to life.

Trade flourished again thanks to tax privileges (free export of sulphur, alum and pumice stone) granted to Lipari by the Angevin and Aragonese kings. In 1544 the Saracen pirate Ariadeno "Barbarossa", allied with the French against Charles V, attacked and sacked Lipari with a fleet of 150 ships after a long siege. He burnt the houses and Cathedral and deported 8,000 people, the entire population, as slaves. There was great dismay in the Christian world. Charles V, the Spanish king of Naples, had stronger walls built around the town and, through tax exemptions and privileges, encouraged the repopulation of Lipari (principally with Spaniards and people from Campania).
However, the islands continued to live in terror of incursions and in 1589 were annexed to the Kingdom of the Two Sicilies. Not until the end of the 1700s, with the end of Turkish piracy, did the town begin to expand again, first under the Spaniards, then under the Bourbons, the Savoias, the Austrians and finally under the Spaniards again, until the unification of Italy.

Lipari Castle

Vulcano is the first island you meet coming from Milazzo, just 12 miles away. Near the port you are struck, both by the beauty of the place, and by the acrid smell of sulphur which fills the air. The phenomenon, which you soon get used to, is due to the "fumaroles", the venting of steam, sulphur and carbon dioxide at a high temperature from the crater or from cracks in the ground. The fumaroles are a reminder that the volcano is still active. The island takes its name from the considerable volcanic activity over thousands of years. Along with Stromboli, it is the only volcano still active in the archipelago, and the youngest (90,000 years compared with the 100,000 years of Stromboli). This island, today invaded by tourists, must have made a great impression on the Greeks and Romans who called it **Terasia** (Hot land), then **Thermessa** (Hot), and dedicated it to the God of Fire, Hephaestus for the Greeks and Vulcan for the Romans, and considered it a holy island (**Hierà**).

The discovery of numerous caves dug in the tuff near the flat land in the south of the island, maybe rocky tombs called **Grotte dei Rossi**, suggests that the holiness of the place derived from the custom of burying the dead near the god Vulcan. A privileged position for the journey into the next world.

We don't know if the forge of the Gods was here, but it is certain that from time immemorial only forced labourers and slaves lived on the island, extracting alum and sulphur. The setting must have been like one of Dante's circles, with the venting of sulphur, which made it difficult to breathe, and periodic volcanic activity which launched incandescent rocks. Mining continued for centuries until it became a full-scale industry under the Bourbons. General Nunziante built roads, houses and factories. When the Bourbons fell, the island was bought by an Englishman, a Mr. **Stevenson**, who continued the work of his predecessors, enlarging the mine and planting vines.

His villa, still called the **"Castello dell'inglese"** is on the plateau of Vulcano, near the mud baths. In 1888 the last eruption took place, which blew out the "plug" made of sedimented magmatic material which had been consolidated by a previous eruption. The Englishman fled, terrified by the shower of blocks of fused magmatic material, "bread-crust bombs", which cooled on contact with the air and cracked up.

The few inhabitants who remained, maybe Stevenson's settlers, dedicated themselves to farming and sheep-rearing on the plateau and fishing in the hamlet of Gelso.

The rest is recent history; decades of silence on a beautiful uninhabited island, until, in 1949, the director **Dieterle** made a film on Vulcano with **Anna Magnani**, and interest in the island was reawakened. Year after year it has become an international tourist destination with the attraction of the volcano, mud baths and clear water.

Vulcano Port

DISCOVERING THE ISLAND

Ferrics and hydrofoils arrive at **Porto di Levante**, but before attempting to climb the volcano, perhaps it is better to get an idea of the place. It is a good idea to reach the top of the **Faraglione di Levante** (36 metres high), to the right of the quay. From here you can see **Vulcanello**, which emerged from the sea in 183 BC following underwater eruptions. It is connected to the island by an isthmus of sand and lava which has created two bays. To the East, you can see the natural **mud baths**, famous even in Roman times for curing rheumatism, arthrosis and skin diseases. It is difficult to resist taking a dip, despite the strong smell. Near the baths the sea water is heated by underwater **"fumaroles"** and the bottom is hot. It is better to go into the water with beach shoes to avoid burning your feet.

"Lying immersed in the bubbling water is a unique experience and gives a great feeling". The fine black volcanic sand distinguishes the eastern beach which is full of bathers and boats. The **sabbie nere** beach is bordered by the **Scoglio delle Sirene** to the left and to the right Vulcanello, in which there is the **Valle dei Mostri**. It takes its name from the strange rock forms shaped by the wind and sea, among black sand dunes. Vulcanello has two extinct craters and thick vegetation.

The best way to visit the rest of the island is to rent a Vespa or moped at the port, from **Campisi** (tel. 9852574) or **Marturano** (tel. 9852419) or use the bus which goes to the **Piano**. From **Porto di Levante**, a tarmacked road leads to the **Piano** and **Gelso**. On the right, after 2 km there is **Monte Lentia**, an extinct volcano, from the top of which you can admire the beautiful, rugged coast from **Caposecco** to **Cala del Formaggio**. After 7 km, you arrive on the high plateau formed by the filling in of the older large crater of the island, along a road surrounded by trees, brooms, vines and pastures in contrast to the

Left: quay with Eastern crag

Above: the natural mud baths

Opposite page: Vulcano and Vulcanello

barren volcano. Here, in neat white houses, live most of the residents. Following a steep path, among capers and vines, you go down to the **Borgo di Gelso**. This is the quietest part of the island, with the **Old Light house** and the lovely beach **Spiaggia dell'Asino**. The inhabitants, farmers and fishermen, have lived for almost a century cultivating black grapes and capers and fishing. In the characteristic restaurants of the hamlet, simple but excellent meals are served.

Two more interesting destinations are: **il vallone della Roja**, a lava abyss which drops straight down to the sea, accessible along a path on the left at Passo del Piano; **Punta Grillo**, accessible on foot along a path from **Piano di Luccia**, after leaving the houses of Piano. From here there is a unique view and you can lunch well in the nearby *trattorie*.

DISCOVERING THE SEA

You can hire boats from **Baia Levante** (Porto di Levante, tel. 9822197) and **Sabbie Nere** (Porto di Ponente, tel 9852379). For diving and tank refilling, **Vulcano Mare** (tel. 9852262). Leaving Porto Levante to sail around the island (28 km), you sail north, following the peninsula of Vulcanello. You can observe the longitudinal crack of the **Crater of Vulcanello**. After passing **Punta Samossà** and **Punta del Roveto**, you reach the **Valle dei Mostri** with its strange rocks. Passing by the Sabbie Nere and the Faraglione delle Sirene you find the spectacular **Cala del Formaggio** and **Mastro Minico** with their unfrequented beaches, divided by lava promontories which stick out into the sea: an extraordinary coast with steep rugged slopes. Rounding **Punta Monaco**, after the promontory **Testa Grossa**, you discover a little bay surrounded by rocks, directly under Monte Lentia. On the left, the shallow sea ringed by cliffs forms the so-called **Bagno delle Vergini**, a natural pool with emerald coloured water.

At the bottom of the flow the **Grotta del Cavallo** opens up. You can go inside, even in small boats, to admire its vault and swim with the sunlight shining on the blue-green water. Perhaps the best time is at sunset. **Capo Secco** with its **Scoglio Quaglietta** is followed by **Spiaggia Lunga** and **Punta Conigliara**, so called because of the large number of rabbits in the area, sheer and horizontal lava formations furrowed by gorges, as far as a low tongue of land on which the **Old Lighthouse**

Opposite page bottom: Eastern beach,

Opposite page above right: "Virgin's bath"

Left: Grotta del Cavallo,above: Coast of Vulcano

stands. Here is the "Scario", the landing-place for Gelso, the Spiaggia dell'Asino and then the beach of Cannitello. A stop here is a must.
You set off again towards **Punta Bandiera.** From the sea you glimpse terraces and farmhouses and just beyond **Punta Molo di Femmina**, while the high **Monte Aria** (an old volcano) dominates the scene.
Next is **Punta del Grillo**, in which a lava flow has created a series of small splendid caves. It is a beautiful place with tricks of the light and a hot water source. After the bastion of **Punta Luccia**, the **Cala Rossa** opens up with great depths, with **Punta Roja** in correspondence to a cliff with the statue of the Little Mermaid.
You follow the northern side of the **Cratere della Forgia Vecchia** with jagged black points and you are back at Porto di Levante. Every day tours round the island take place for those who prefer organised trips (**Sen** tel. 9812341).

Top: Gelso Lighthouse

Bottom: Gelso village

ISOLA di VULCANO
N
Punta di Levante
Punta S. Giuseppe
Punta di Jacopo
Umazzo
Capistello
Scogliera Sotto il Monte
la Forbice
S. Lazzaro
Falcone
S. Salvatore
Punta di Costa
Osservatorio Geofisico
Scoglio della Secca
le Formiche
Capparo
Punta del Perciato
Sponda di Vinci
Pietralunga
Punta della Crapazza
Scoglio Quadro di S. Giuseppe
Pietra Menalda
Sponda Lena
Punta del Roveto
Punta Liscio
Punta Samossà
Vulcanello
Punta dello Scoglietto
Porto di Ponente
Cappello di Bonanno
Punta Cala del Formaggio
Cala del Formaggio
Capo Grosso
Sabbie Nere
Sorgenti Termali
Fumarole
Porto di Levante
Scoglio di Mastro Minico
Cala di Mastro Minico
il Faraglione
Punta di Mastro Minico
Punte Nere
Punta del Monaco
C. Lentia
Punta Lùccia
Punta Roia
Forgia Vecchia
Punta della Sciara del Monte
Monte Lentia
Sorgente Termale
Valle della Roia
Caruggi
Gran Cratere la Fossa di Vulcano
Testa Grossa
Monte Lùccia
Capo Grillo
Grotta del Cavallo
Punta Argia
Punta di Capo Secco
Pietra Quaglietto
Scoglio di Capo Secco
Vallonazzo
Grotta dei Palizzi
Punta Quadrara
Monte Molineddo
Punta Lunga
Cava di Pomice
Spiaggia Lunga
Passo del Piano
Piano Grotte dei Rossi
Piano di Lùccia
Sciara di Lunga
Monte Rosso
Cugni di Molinello
Cugno Petroso
Chiappe Lisce
Grotta dei Pisani
Sciara Fossa di Miglio
la Schicciola
Piano d'Alighieri
Menichedda
il Cardo
C. Villante
Punta Molo di Femmina
Monte Sareceno
Monte Aria o Scoglio del Cardo
Punta di Cugno Lungo
il Piano
la Sommata
Capo Secco
Portella della Trovatina
Cugno Chiatto
Scoglio dell'Arpa
Punta del Rosario
Grotta dell'Abate
Scoglio Conigliara
Punta Conigliara
La Portella
Case Petrulla
Punta Bandiera o dell'Aria
T. del Corvo
Case Amendola
Pennata
Sciara dei Pisani
Sciara delle Felicicchie
Case Carnevali
Scogliazzo
Case Buongiorno
Quadrara
Punta dell'Ufala
Case Scolaticci
Punta dell'Asino
Punta del Mortaro
Gelso
Faro Vecchio
Sponda Lena
Faro Nuovo

THE CLIMB TO THE CRATER

A visitor who arrives at the port of Vulcano can't help noticing the close contact between the crater and the built-up areas.
The contact is not only physical, the development of a town on the slopes of an active volcano, but much deeper and spiritual. The livelihood of the islanders and their very lives depend on that volcanic cone, so close and so quiet for more than a century.

An excursion to the crater is a walk not to be missed. It is a unique sensation and lets you discover an unimaginable world. From Porto di Levante you walk along the road to Piano and on the left, after 150 metres, there is a path which leads to the crater. The climb, easy at first, continues with bends among high red rocks and broom plants.
The path gets more difficult and uneven and crosses a barren landscape which leads to a large dark area of level ground. You climb up gradually and, as you go up, your sensations and the scenery change considerably and you see all the other islands.
You discover that Vulcano is an island rich in vegetation, with deep valleys caused by volcanic activity, and covered with scented brooms, the first plants able to take root on recent volcanic soil. Your arrival on the edge of the crater gives you a series of strong sensations, which are repeated even in someone who often comes here in the course of his work.
It is difficult to imagine, and even more to explain, how you feel on a narrow path, with a view of the sea and islands on one side, and on the other, the heart of a living mountain giving off steam, heat and hisses coloured with sulphur. The awareness that, in the past, from the crater forces of nature capable of changing the shape of the countryside have broken out, makes you respect and fear this place pulsating with life.

Dr. Franco Italiano
Vulcanologist

SHOPPING

The "life" of Vulcano is concentrated around Porto Levante and its square. At any time you can have a granita at **Remigio** and in the evening you can meet for an ice-cream at **Enrico** or **Zammara**, taking an evening stroll past the shops. **"L'arte della casa"**, dug out of the Faraglione, offers locally produced objects and jewellery, at **"I Gioielli del Mare"** you can choose from shells, minerals and gold jewellery, at **Adriana Salvini** you can find broom essence and at **Chantal** you can buy objects in gold or coral. Sicilian pottery at **"La Ginestra"** and **"Il Forno"**, at the **Vecchio Castello**, lava objects. Finally the grocer's **Da Giovannino**, selling ricotta, olives, capers, malmsey and the famous pecorino.

RESTAURANTS AND TRATTORIE

In the paradise of fish, you can fish by day and observe the underwater world by night with the "lampara", just arrange it with the fishermen.
In any case fish, very fresh, is found in the restaurants of the island dressed with capers, olives and tomatoes.

AT THE SABBIE NERE

- LES SABLES NOIRS: Luxurious with views of the other islands. Local dishes and international cuisine.
- EOLIAN HOTEL: Good views, near the black beach, in a mediterranean garden. Recommended: the grouper "a ghiotta".
- CONTI: Right near the beach; bar, restaurant, pizzeria.
- MARI DEL SUD: High above the western beach, fish based menu: scorpion fish, swordfish and lobsters. A touch of oriental cuisine.
- A ZAMMARA: Near the beach; pizzas, "schiacciate" and a little music.

AT PORTO DI LEVANTE

- DA VINCENZINO: Spaghetti "alla Vincenzino" with capers, prawns and tomato, grilled swordfish.
- DA MAURIZIO: Homemade pasta with courgettes, curry risotto and swordfish skewers.
- IL PALMENTO: Good pizzas from a wood-burning oven, in the garden of an old mill and many typical Sicilian dishes.
- IL CAIMANO: Bar, restaurant, pizzeria with a panoramic terrace. Excellent fish dishes.
- L'ORSA MAGGIORE: In a pine wood at Sotto Lentia, near the Sabbie Nere (tel. 9852018).
- DON PIRICUDDU: Spaghetti with sardines and grouper "alla marinara".
- LANTERNA BLU: Pizzas and traditional Sicilian dishes.

AT PIANO

- IL DIAVOLO DEI POLLI: Meat roasted on a giant spit, excellent rabbit and lamb.
- MARIA TINDARA: This inn offers tagliatelle "alla vulcanara", lamb and rabbit.
- BELVEDERE: Pasta "al belvedere" or "alla sora Maria" and goat.

Above: Black sands beach and Vulcanello

Left: characteristic tomatoes "a scocca"

Opposite page: sunset over the crater

AT GELSO

- DA GAETANO: Near the lighthouse, 5 minutes from Gelso beach. Simple and genuine cuisine, sea-food like fresh marinated anchovies, barbecued hors d'oeuvres.
- PINA MANIACI
- TONY MANIACI

The fashionable place for aperitifs is **"Al Castello"**, and there are two night clubs: the **"Rocce Rosse"** at Vulcanello and the **"Piro Piro"**, both overlooking the bay of Porto Ponente. There is live music at the Hotel Faraglione and at Remigio.

WHERE TO STAY

On the island there are two travel agencies, **Reguzzoni** (tel. 9852149) and **Thermessa Viaggi** (tel. 9852230) and 8 agencies rent out houses and accommodation around the island: **Vulcano Blù** at the port (tel. 9852293), **Immobiliare Muscarà** (tel. 9852033), **Multivacanze Immobiliare** (tel 9852184), **Paguro** (tel: 9852226), **Residence al Porto** (tel. 9852059), **Sea House Service** (tel. 9852219), **Natoli Carmelo** (tel. 9852059), **Residence Lanterna Bleu** (tel. 9852178).

HOTELS

- LES SABLES NOIRS ♥♥♥♥: The first hotel built at the "Sabbie Nere", with 33 rooms and a luxurious garden (tel. 9850 pbx).
- EOLIAN HOTEL ♥♥♥: 100 rooms in Eolian style surrounded by green and very near the sea (tel. 9852151).
- ARCIPELAGO ♥♥♥: At Vulcanello, with a large swimming pool, very near the sea (tel. 9852002).
- ALBERGO CONTI ♥♥: 62 rooms and a lovely garden near the beach of the Sabbie Nere (tel. 9852012)
- GARDEN VULCANO ♥♥: At Porto di Ponente, characteristic hibiscus and bougainvillea on every terrace (tel: 9852069).
- MARI DEL SUD ♥♥: Panoramic, at Porto di Ponente (tel. 9852201).
- FARAGLIONE ♥♥: At the port, near the quay, with piano bar in the evening (tel. 9852054).
- ORSA MAGGIORE ♥♥: At Porto di Ponente (tel. 9852018).
- ROJAS BAHIA HOTEL ♥♥: At Porto di Ponente (tel. 9852080).
- AGOSTINO ♥: At Porto di Levante (tel. 9852342).

Rooms for rent: At Porto di Levante, **La Giara** (tel. 9852229) and **Sipione Holiday House** (tel. 9852034); at Piano, **Maria Tindara** (tel. 9852063).

THE EOLIAN ISLANDS AND THE CINEMA

The "face of the Eolians", the emblematic title chosen by Panaria Films to illustrate the pictures of Francesco Alliata, Renzo Avanzo, Quintino di Napoli and Pietro Moncada, could be the leitmotif of the love story between the cinema and these islands. It is undeniably a question of love at first sight for these black lava and white pumice cliffs, for the arrogance and wildness of nature, which is, at the same time, prickly like a cactus, but warm and passionate like the flowering brooms.

Foreign travellers who visited the islands in the 18th and 19th centuries, in search of adventure and discovery, had no influence at all on local customs, but nonetheless collected images and evidence which are very useful to us today, in reconstructing the recent history of the islands. The first strong social and cultural influence came from political internees in the 20's and 30's. Perhaps for the first time, an interpersonal relationship was established between "foreigners" and islanders, fruitful and important for both: for those who realised that beyond the cliffs and the sea exists a complex and ancient civilization and for those who learnt of a new cultural dimension.

Nitti, Lussu, Rosselli and Malaparte left a deep impression on the Eolians, giving the islanders a cultural depth and literary dimension which proved to be another step towards the transformation which would change the face of the islands. An important role was played in this transformation by the cinema which, after the documentaries by Alliata, Maraini and Moncada, began to invest energy and resources in a series of productions which suddenly enlivened these "cliffs lost in the blue".

In 1949 Dieterle and Rossellini began filming "Vulcano" and "Stromboli" at almost the same time; scriptwriters, costume designers and others fussed around the stars of the moment Anna Magnani and Ingrid Bergman, who scowled at each other, from one coast to another: one with popular passionateness and the other with nordic arrogance.

Never had there been such disturbance to the peace of those lava stones and black sandy paths; but, in reality, the cinema managed to say little or nothing about the people, people with faces hollowed out by the wind and the salt, the men bent over the vines and fishing nets, the busy and serious women, with large industrious hands and large black intense eyes, the children, thin and agile like wild animals.

In the newspaper reports of those years the myth of the wild island was born: but the men, their culture, history and marvellous dignity were of less interest to the scandal mongers than the loves of Ingrid and the fury of Nannarella.

All of this in the frame of a continually stormy sea and a volcano in all its splendour with powerful lava flows at sunset.

Left: short stop behind the stage of the film "Vulcano"

Opposite page: Anna Magnani

Yet the men were there and gradually their relationship with nature, the land and the sea changed.
Slowly but inexorably, the men of the Eolians became aware that life is also "elsewhere": beyond the timeless spell of the cliffs lost in the sea and still inviolate.
Slowly but inexorably, like an unhappy destiny (the same one which violated the rain forests and coral reefs and decimated the New Zealand Maoris and Amazonian Tupis), they invented new opportunities, another life.
The large knotted hands, which used to tend vines, to pickaxe pumice and weave nets, turned to mixing cement to build roads and houses. Then unexpected riches arrived after the great wave of emigration, and noise and chaos after centuries of silence.
Through the cinema it is possible to reconstruct the most recent history of the islands: from the myth of the wild island of "Vulcano" (1949) and "Stromboli" (1949), to Antonioni's "L'Avventura" (1960) which represents man's search for himself, up to the dazzling splendour of the Taviani brothers' "Kaos" (1983) an unforgettable fresco of indigo and white tones.
Nostalgia for so much silent but overshadowing beauty, unconsciously arrogant, hard and mysterious, justifies Moretti's choice of these "islands", excessive and chaotic, hybrid and contrasting: microcosms symbolic of the absolute, inexorable madness of our time, which destroys not only with hydrocarbons and nuclear weapons, but also and above all, with uniformity and forgetfulness.
Another example of nostalgia is "Il Postino" with Massimo Troisi, made at Pollara on Salina, just before the actor's death. But in this case the nostalgia has a different taste, or rather sound: the unceasing sound of the waves, the intriguing rustling of the leaves, the mysterious beating of life within the womb.
It is the nostalgia of those who discover the meaning of life just before it ends; of those who look at death in the knowledge that everything passes away, without ever ending completely; because man's worth is in the message he leaves to his children and in the memory of his friends, and in the discovery of the poetry that each of us has inside which can be reawakened by a breath.
The punishment, writes Mario Luzzi, is to endure beyond this moment. Troisi succeeded.

Tilde Paino
Nino Paino

LIPARI

Lipari is the largest and most heavily populated island of the archipelago. The town is spread out under the imposing Castle rock, the ancient Greek acropolis, and along the bays of Marina Corta and Marina Lunga, to the north and south. The houses climb up under the ramparts and via Garibaldi follows them around, from piazza Mazzini to the lovely Marina Corta. This is the usual meeting-place, with crowded bars and ice-cream parlours La Vela, Il Gabbiano, Al Pescatore, with tables outside and big colourful umbrellas and the Caffè del Porto (we suggest you try the granite, all of them).
Marina Corta is connected by an isthmus to the peninsula where the church of the Anime del Purgatorio stands and where the hydrofoils arrive. Jetties have been built which have rather changed the natural look of the place. However, even today, especially out of the tourist season, it still retains the charm of a fishing village. The fishermen came here from Acitrezza at the beginning of the century and their multi-coloured boats are drawn out of the water, in the square, with the nets waiting to be repaired. The statue of San Bartolo, patron of Lipari, welcomes the tourists who find themselves surrounded by shops selling guide-books, post-

cards and souvenirs.
The ferries arrive at Marina Lunga, in the port of Sottomonastero. Lipari or Meligunis, as the Greeks called it because of its mild climate, has a surprising variety of scenery due to its geographical complexity. Twelve volcanoe's have shaped the island over thousands of years. Its volcanic origin is evident in Valle Muria, with its red rocks, and on the north-east coast covered by a vast flow of pumice, which hides Roman ruins of the 4th century AD. On this white mountain three flows of obsidian criss-cross, the Forgia Vecchia, the Rocche

Rosse and the most ancient one Canneto. Pumice and obsidian, black and white, are both glassy and made of silicon but differ regarding specific weight, the way the eruption and cooling of the magma happened, acidity and viscosity. The plates and points produced with the precious obsidian determined the wealth of Lipari before the Bronze Age, as they were goods to exchange with peoples who didn't have them.
Today, the pumice deposits are spread over eight square kilometres and are the second resource of the island after tourism. For more than a century pumice has been exploited for its various uses in the tanning of hides, in building, and as a coating and abrasive.

DISCOVERING THE ISLAND

After a short stop at Marina Corta, you can set off on a visit to the many lovely corners of Lipari.
On the left stands the bell tower of the church of San Giuseppe, which is reached by a hill with the same name, passing the beautiful pottery shop "di Stefano Panza", the Chitarra bar and the restaurant "Il Pirata". Continuing to the right we reach the Hotel Meligunis and then the Piazza delle Arti e dei Mestieri with its realistic murals.

Opposite page top: Castle rock, opposite page bottom: Panorama of Lipari

Above: Marina Corta and the church of Anime del Purgatorio

Right: Marina Corta and S. Giuseppe hill

It's a pleasure to wander around the maze of alleys. Just behind San Giuseppe is the 16th century chapel of San Bartolomeo, wonderful in its simplicity. Nearby the Martino bakery produces sesame biscuits, excellent when dipped in malmsey. From here the road leads to the beach at Porto delle Genti, also called "Portinente" in Sicilian because, being exposed to all winds, it is useless, except when there is dead calm.

Corso Vittorio Emanuele, the old Roman decuman, is still the main street. In the summer months it is always lively, full of tourists and locals. You can go shopping or just take an evening stroll past the rows of shops, agencies and bars. Among the many things on sale, malmsey and capers are the most common. However, it is difficult to find a good bottle of malmsey because the demand far exceeds the supply. On the Corso there is the small piazza Monfalcone, with the confectioner's Subba and the restaurant La Piazzetta, both with tables outside, and Avant Garde with its granite and home-made ice-creams. There is also Belletti, a good book shop and the stationer's Paino. For snacks and pizzas, there are the bakeries Il Fornaretto and Gentile. The antique shop Buceti is worth a visit, as well as Grey's jeweller's, the souvenir shop Raffaele and handmade lace and embroidery at Franco Giunta's shop. For information you can call the Tourist Information Office. Nearby, in the Hotel Oriente you can visit an art and craft collection, run by Edoardo Bongiorno: agricultural and handicraft implements used in the last two centuries,

along with locks, bolts, blacksmiths' and carpenters' tools, scales, typewriters, coffee machines, a Sicilian cart, old tools and lots of old prints. Nearby, there is the Archaeological Park of contrada Diana with its vast necropolis which, unfortunately, has been closed to the public for a long time. On via XXIV Maggio, on the corner of Corso Vittorio Emanuele, you'll see chains of red peppers, onions, garlic, capers and dried tomatoes. "Zia Lina", as she is affectionately called, produces and sells the produce and jars of conserves, displayed on a table.

Opposite, the Spada brothers make clay reproductions of Greek theatre masks, of which a large collection was found on Lipari.

Via Garibaldi is a series of artisans' shops and restaurants, for example the Oasi, with good quality craft products and souvenirs, Mirella with clothing and pareos [beach-wraps] in Positano style, Esse Più for sandwiches and typical Eolian produce, the handmade clothing workshop "La Pecora Nera" and the antique shop China.

In Piazza Mazzini, where the Town Hall is situated, you can find the church of Sant' Antonio, the Turmalin disco, the Blue Moon restaurant and the best-known restaurant on the island, Filippino, which also produces liqueurs and sesame biscuits. From here you can get to the Castle rock and the Museum.

Opposite page bottom: characteristic murals in the piazzetta delle Arti e dei Mestieri

Opposite page top: "Zia Lina" and her wares in via XXIV Maggio: top of page: alleyways. Left: shop in via Garibaldi, above: terracotta reproductions of Greek theatre masks

THE CASTLE

The first destination of our itinerary is visible from all over the town because it rises above it with its imposing sixteenth century walls. It is the natural fortress of the **Castle** rock, a geological structure of volcanic origin, which dominates the two landing places of the island and has been continuously inhabited for six thousand years.

Every era has left its own mark: from neolithic times to the Greek acropolis, from the Roman town to the Norman one, right up to the present fortifications of the Spanish town which hide the remains of previous walls.

You enter the Castle from piazza Mazzini at the end of via Garibaldi.

The Norman fortification, built at the time of Ruggero II, protected the entire northern side of the rock. The entrance is a gate tower, which includes 23 rows of blocks from the **Greek tower** of the early **fourth century** BC.

The **Norman gate** leads into a tunnel whose exit was protected in times of danger by a portcullis and an embrasure. You pass through a short tunnel with ogival arches in neogothic style, constructed in the 19th century, and arrive at another imposing tower, maybe part of late Roman or early mediaeval fortifications.

Another gate, probably of the Aragonese era (19th century), with a large coat of arms painted on the architrave leads into via del Castello. Since 1954 the **Eolian Archaeological Museum** has been based here. We have indicated on the map of the castle the various buildings that make up the museum complex and which can be visited from 9 a.m. to 1 p.m. and 3 p.m. to 6 p.m. The whole castle zone contains important traces of the past, both in the open air in archaeological digs, and inside the pavilions.

On the right the first church is **Santa Caterina**, 17th-18th century, now closed to worship. Further on there is the small **Chiesa dell'Addolorata** with a baroque facade whose foundation goes back to the 16th century, with beautiful wooden altars and gilded stuccoes; the large **Chiesa dell'Immacolata**, built in 1747, with a smooth facade. To the south of the chiesa S. Caterina, and in front of the Immacolata, there are two **archaeological areas** with the remains of huts relating to the **Bronze Age** and parts of the Hellenistic and Roman towns (a "decumano" or main street, crossed by "cardines" secondary streets). Near the archaeological areas, information boards show

Above: Norman Castle gate

Left: old walls and sarcophagi at the Archaeological Museum

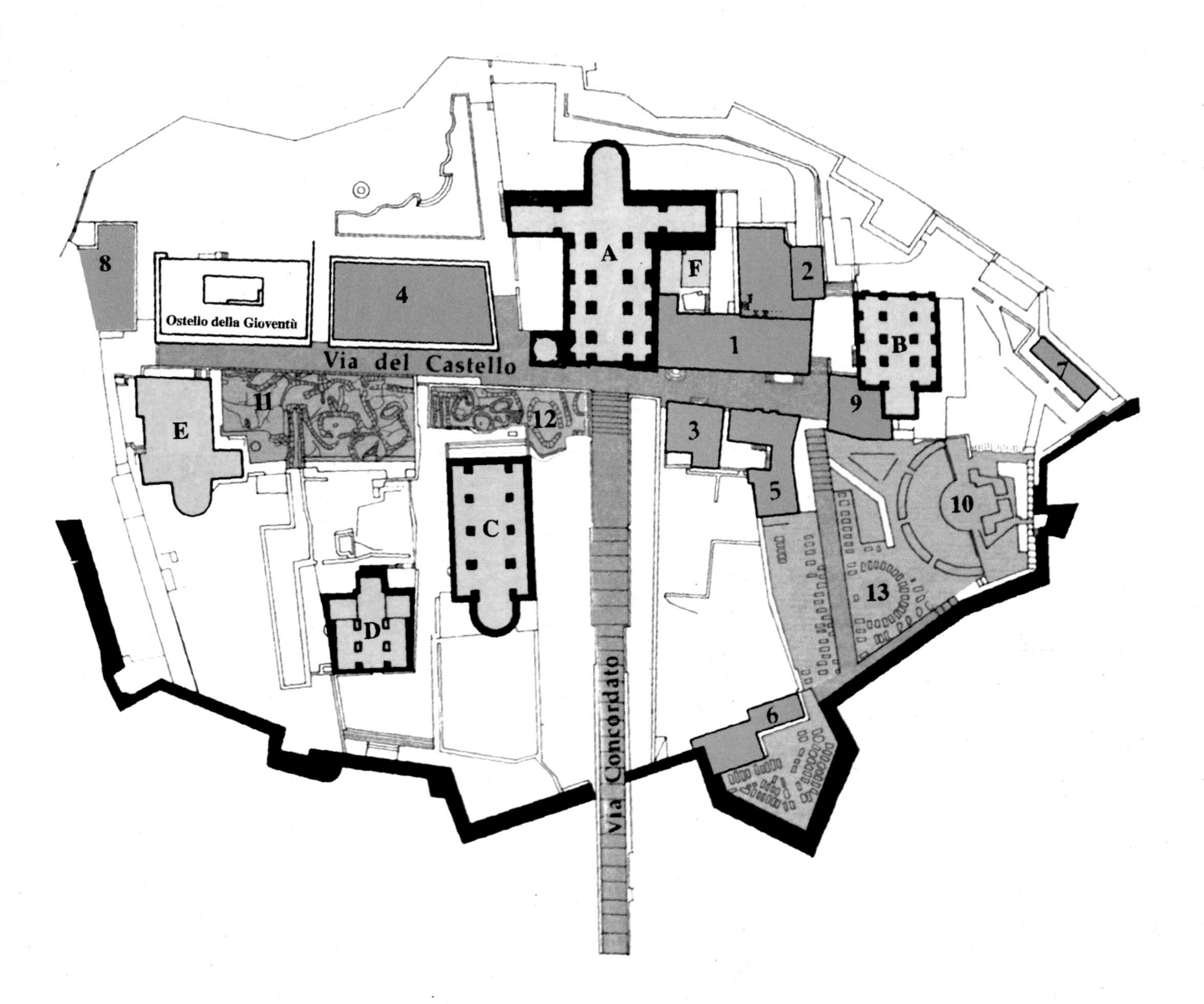

Lipari Castle and the Eolian Archaeological Museum

Museum buildings and open areas

1 Prehistoric section; Rooms 1 - 10
2 Epigraphic Pavilion and garden
3 Smaller islands section; Rooms 11 - 15
4 Classical section; Rooms 16 - 27
5 Volcanological section
6 Quaternary Paleontology
7 Large carthenware store
8 Administration and offices
9 Library and Scientific Section
10 Open air theatre
11/12 Excavation trenches with layers of archaeological remains: huts from four Bronze Age villages and parts of the Hellenistic-Roman town.
13 Archaeological Park (Sarcophagi of Greek age found in the necropolis of Diana)

Churches

A) S. Bartholomew Cathedral (12 th - 19 th century)
B) Maria SS delle Grazie Church (18 th century)
C) Immacolata Church (18 th century)
D) Addolorata Church (16 th - 18 th century)
E) S. Caterina Church (16 th - 18 th century)
F) Norman Monastery Cloister (12 th century)

the series of chronological phases, with maps divided into different coloured sections.

Next to the excavations is the stairway called **Via del Concordato**, built in the early 1900s to provide a direct connection between the Cathedral and the town. The stairway has, however, completely changed the original layout of the rock, damaging the archaeological stratifications.

At the bottom of the stairway, to the right, there is the **archaeological park** where the Greek sarcophagi from the necropolis of contrada Diana have been put. In 1976 an open-air theatre was built, based on a Greek model, with wonderful natural scenery. It is an oasis of peace and serenity.

A fifth church, **Santa Maria delle Grazie**, was built in the 17th and 18th centuries on the site of an already existing place of worship.

The **Cathedral** of San Bartolomeo rises up majestically with the bell tower in neo-baroque style. Seriously damaged in 1544 during the incursion by the pirate **Barbarossa**, it was completely rebuilt and decorated several times. Of the Norman church with one nave it retains the transept

Left: entrance to Archeological Museum

Below: cloister of ancient Norman Abbey

Opposite page: Cathedral of St. Bartholomew and the Concordate stairway

and the presbytery. Rebuilding began in the 1500s in **gothic style** and was completed in the 1600s in baroque style. The interior has a nave and two aisles with cross-vaults, decorated with frescoes of the 1700s showing events from the Old Testament. Behind the altar there is a silver statue of San Bartolomeo from the 1700s.

From inside you can visit the lovely **cloister** of the old **Norman Abbey**. Only three sides of it remain because one was swallowed up by the right hand aisle of the Church after the extension.

The ambulatories of the cloister are divided into spans with cross-vaults and have columns with Doric capitals, recovered from the entrance halls of Graeco-Roman houses destroyed by the Saracens, and columns with smooth shafts and capitals decorated with stylised leaves, drawings of birds, monsters, doves, etc. The cloister opens onto an interior garden. The later construction of the Bishop's Palace used the spaces of the portico, walling up the columns and capitals and thereby preserving them for 800 years. They had been forgotten until the recent discovery and restoration which brought back a work of art.

Right: Spanish fortifications with view of Marina Corta

Below: Greek-style open-air theatre on the Castle Rock

Opposite page: Archaeological digs at Lipari Castle

The Eolian Museum, established in 1954 by Luigi Bernabò Brea and Madeleine Cavalier, exhibits artefacts from the intensive digs carried out by the two archaeologists in the Eolian islands, from the 1940's to the present day. It is housed in several buildings on the Castle Rock of Lipari.

It is a "living" museum in constant and direct touch with the local community (the increase and development of its collections and exhibitions, as well as its infrastructure, are almost continuous), and so it is dedicated to the continuation of archaeological research.

The exhibition, though scientifically rigorous, is designed to educate and the clear layout makes it easy to visit even for non-experts.

The historical reconstructions using original pieces from the digs are particularly effective with the public (the late Bronze Age necropolis of Piazza Monfalcone on Lipari, the prehistoric and protogreek necropoles of Milazzo, part of the Greek necropolis on Lipari).

The explanatory texts which accompany the exhibition are on two levels: red texts in Italian and English with essential information, for a quick but informative visit, and more detailed texts in black print, which are in the process of being translated into English.

In the various sections the public can consult information points with interactive texts, containing a wide range of information and detailed explanations on the archaeological and monumental development of the Castle and all the exhibits at the museum.

The visit begins in the **prehistoric section**, inside the Bishop's palace, built in the early 18th century, incorporating the remains of part of the Norman monastery of the 12th century. It is dedicated to the various prehistoric cultures which succeeded one another on the island of Lipari, from the first human presence of the 5th millennium BC (middle neolithic) and, in the last room, the topography of Greek Lipara and the late Roman town.

On the upper floor Room I: first phase of the Eolian neolithic, probably the last centuries of the 5th millennium BC.

Settlement on the heights of Castellaro Vecchio in the western part of the island (about 400m above sea level).

As well as evidence of the obsidian industry (blades,

cones, fragments) which also characterises later cultures of the Eolian neolithic, there is "stentinillian" style pottery, decorated with incisions or imprints.

Second phase of the Eolian neolithic: first centuries of the 4th millennium BC.

First human presence on the Castle Rock of people other than those settled at Castellaro Vecchio: three-coloured painted pottery, brown pottery different from that of Castellaro Vecchio, but similar to that found in Yugoslavia or Albania.

Room II. Third phase of the Eolian neolithic: around 3500 BC.

New settlement on the Castle Rock, characterised by pottery with intricate spiral patterns in the Serra d'Alto style.

Upper Neolithic. Last centuries of the 4th millennium BC.

Contrada Diana is inhabited. Extensive evidence of the

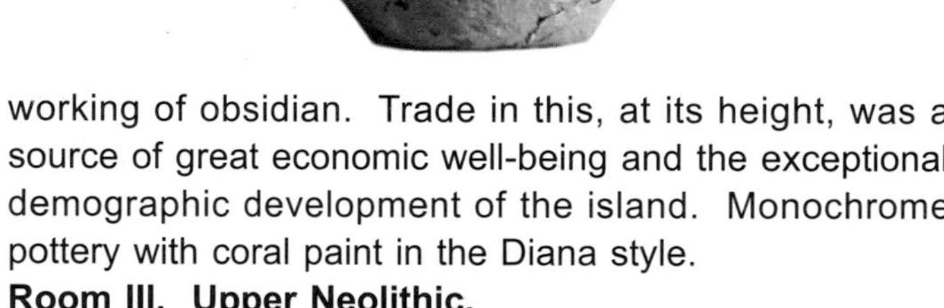

working of obsidian. Trade in this, at its height, was a source of great economic well-being and the exceptional demographic development of the island. Monochrome pottery with coral paint in the Diana style.

Room III. Upper Neolithic.

More pottery from Contrada Diana.

First phase of the Eneolithic: first centuries of 3rd millennium BC.

Settlement of Spatarella on the western slopes of Monte Giardino. Settlement of the Castle Rock.

Pottery in Diana style with influences

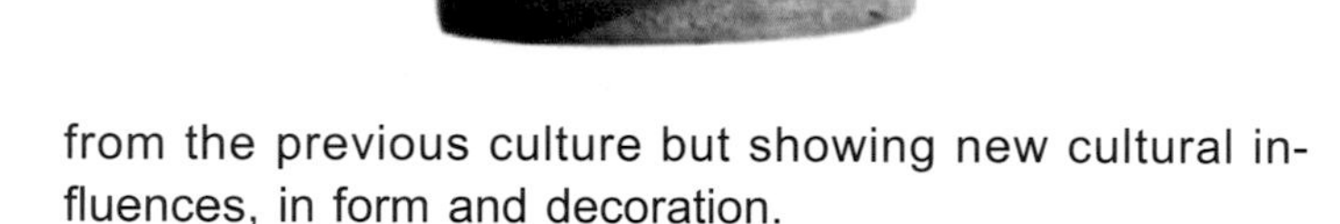

from the previous culture but showing new cultural influences, in form and decoration.

Waste from the fusion of copper from the Castle, first important evidence of local metal working.

Reconstruction, in two showcases, of a stratagraphic section of a trench from the Castle digs with the succession of various levels of settlement, from the middle neolithic to the historical age.

Room IV. Middle phase of the Eneolithic. Around the middle of the 3rd millennium BC.

Culture of Piano Quartara (from the settlement of the same name on Panarea).

Settlement of contrada Diana. Pottery in the Piano Quartara style which shows contact with the late eneolithic cultures of Sicily.

Room V. Early Bronze Age. Culture of Capo Graziano. First phase: first centuries of the 2nd millennium BC.

Piana di Lipari inhabited with crematorium at Contrada Diana.

Room VI. Early Bronze Age.

Evolved and final phases of the culture of Capo Graziano: 18th-15th century BC.

Previous page: archaeological zone next to the Museum

Above: Middle neolithic, three-coloured pottery phase, early 4th mill. B.C.

Right: traditional protoelladic vase shapes, early Bronze Age 2nd mill. B.C.

Opposite page: lamp, cup and jug Ausonio II 11th-12th cent. B.C.

The Castle Rock is inhabited: huts of "green phase" (for this settlement and the successive ones of the Bronze Age, we refer to the colours which differentiate the phases of the planimetry and the sections on the information boards and in the two trenches of the Castle dig and inside the museum). Pottery in the Capo Graziano style, from the first half of the 16th century BC. Painted pottery of protomycenean Aegean import.

Middle Bronze Age. Milazzese culture: end of the 15th - first half of the 13th century BC.

Village on the Castle Rock: huts of the "red phase". Milazzese style pottery with shapes and decorations typologically similar to those of the Sicilian culture of Thaspos.

Painted Mycenaean pottery (Mycenaean IIIA and early IIIB).

Marks and stamps of Aegean type on local pottery.

Ground Floor. Room VII. Late Bronze Age. Ausonio I: 1270 BC circa, late 12th century BC.

Village on the Castle Rock: huts of the "light blue phase". Pottery with shapes and decorative typologies similar to those of the Late Appeninico of mainland Italy; few fragments of painted pottery of the Mycenaean IIIB and C; bronze objects (in particular fibulas) and various instruments (scythes, saws).

Ausonio II. Initial phase: late 12th - early 11th century BC.

Crematorium and necropolis of Piazza Monfalcone: objects in bronze (fibulas, brooches etc.), precious necklaces in Baltic amber, precious stones, glassy material, crystal pearls of gold rock.

Room VIII. Ausonio II. Late 12th - 10th century BC.

Village on the Castle Rock: huts of the "blue phase". Pottery typologically similar to those of the "protovillanoviana" culture of mainland Italy, of which examples must have been imported with geometrical decoration; pottery decorated in the style of the Sicilian Pantalica II - Cassibile culture (10th century BC); numerous nuraghic pottery from Sardinia; rare fragments of the Mycenaean IIIC.

Room IX. Final phases of Ausonio II.

Pottery remains of the final phase of Ausonio II (late 10th century BC) coming from the layer of destruction of the huts of the Castle village.

Room X. Topography of Graeco-Roman Lipàra.

In the western wall is included a large stretch of the wall of the Norman monastery which uses blocks of lava stone from the Greek city walls of the 4th century BC.

"Bothros" (votive well) complex of the sanctuary of Aeolus from the Acropolis. Circular cover of the "Bothros" in lava stone with handle in the form of a crouched lion (mid 6th century BC); among the many votive offerings (pottery remains, terracotta statues etc. dated between

the mid 6th and late 5th century BC, the pitcher with Greek inscription dedicated to Aeolus and the large "deinos" (jug for pouring out water and wine) of Attic production, with black figures by the artist of Antimenes with the exploits of Hercules and Theseus on the outer rim (circa 530 BC).

On show in the same room are Graeco-Roman age pottery, especially from the Acropolis; a marble head of an acrolite (statue with the body in marble and garments in bronze) of the late 5th century BC; bronze coins from Graeco-Roman Lipàra from the late 5th to 1st century BC; a male statue draped in marble from the late 4th - early 3rd century BC from the Acropolis; a marble statue of a girl from the Imperial Roman age from Contrada Diana.

From Room X you pass into the epigraphic garden, bordered to the north and east by the structure of the Norman monastery, where sarcophagi and funeral stands are exhibited. They are in lava stone with the name in Greek and come from the Graeco-Roman necropolis of Contrada Diana.

On the southern side you enter the Epigraphic Pavilion, in a building that exhibits numerous funeral stands and stones from the necropolis, from the 5th to 1st century BC.

SMALLER ISLANDS SECTION. In front of the Prehistoric Section.

Dedicated to the prehistoric settlements of the smaller islands of the Eolian archipelago, from the middle neolithic to the middle Bronze Age.

Room XI.

There are large pots of the Milazzese age from the Portella settlement on Salina.

Room XII. Neolithic and eneolithic.

Materials from the oval hut of Rinicedda di Leni on Salina, belonging to a middle-neolithic settlement (last centuries of the 5th millennium BC) contemporary of the older settlement of Lipari, at Castellaro Vecchio: "stentinellian" style pottery.

Artefacts from the upper neolithic age (second half of the 4th millennium BC) from Salina and Panarea.

Middle-eneolithic. Culture of Pianoconte.

Stromboli: settlement at Serra Fareddu.

Upper-eneolithic. Culture of Piano Quartara.

Panarea: settlement at Piano Quartara.

Salina: huts at Serro Brigadiere and Serro dell'Acqua, three vases from a tomb at Malfa.

Early Bronze Age. First phases of the culture of Capo Graziano (20th -19th century BC).

Filicudi:

1) Huts of the coastal village of Piano di Porto: pottery.

2) Funeral and burial objects from the rock on the slopes of the Montagnola di Piano Graziano.

Room XIII. Early Bronze Age. Culture of Capo Graziano.

Filicudi: Capo Graziano. Settlement of Montagnola (probably 19th - 18th century BC). Pottery in the Capo Graziano style, various fictile objects, a form of fusion in stone for the manufacture of bronze instruments; from the early 16th century BC painted Aegean pottery (Mycenaean I and II).

Panarea: vases from the Capo Graziano age, probably from a votive shrine at Punta Peppe Maria.

Alicudi: fragments of the Capo Graziano style from Contrada Fucile.

Left: archaeological digs at Capo Graziano, Filicudi

Opposite page: amphoras from shipwrecks

Room XIV. Early Bronze Age. Culture of Capo Graziano.
Stromboli: settlement of San Vincenzo.
Middle Bronze Age: Milazzese culture.
Filicudi: Montagnola di Capo Graziano. Settlement levels of the Milazzese culture superimposed on the village of the Capo Graziano culture: Milazzese style pottery, fragments of painted Aegean pottery of the Mycenaean III A I.
Room XV.
Salina: tip with pottery materials from the early and middle Bronze Age settlements of Serro dei Cianfi (culture of Capo Graziano and successive Milazzese culture).
Middle Bronze Age: Milazzese culture
Salina: settlement established on the ridge of Contrada Portella (oval huts), Milazzese style pottery, much with potters' stamps; mesoappeninic pottery from the Italian mainland; precious stone necklaces of Mycenaean origin.
Panarea: settlement of Capo Milazzese (oval huts, one square): Milazzese style pottery with numerous potters' marks, painted Aegean pottery of the Mycenaean III A and B, mesoappenminic pottery, form of fusion in sandstone for bronze strips.
CLASSICAL ARCHAEOLOGICAL SECTION
In a building of the ex-Fascist internment camp, rebuilt after the war and recently enlarged.
Ground Floor.
MILAZZO ARCHAEOLOGY SECTION
Exhibits many artefacts from the digs at Milazzo in the 1950's.
Room XVI.
Reconstruction of the trench from the dig of the middle Bronze Age necropolis of Predio Caravello, belonging to the Milazzese culture (1430 -1270 BC): burial with the body huddled in large pots.
Room XVII.
Protovillanovian necropolis.
Reconstructions, with the original stratigraphy, of a crematorium of the protovillanovian necropolis of the isthmus: 12th century BC, contemporary of the final phase of Ausonio I of Lipari and early Ausonio II. The funeral rite and the form of the urns, inside chambers lined with gravel or in baskets of lithic sheets, correspond to those of the so-called protovillanovian necropolis of the Italian mainland.
Room XVIII.
Archaic Greek necropolis of Mylai.
Mylai (Milazzo) was founded around 716 BC as a fortress of the Calcidese colony (founded by Greek colonisers of Calcide in Eubea) of Zancle, today Messina.
The archaic necropolis, established on the isthmus on the same site as the protovillanovian one, is also composed of cremated remains (some reconstructed in the previous room) with ashes in vascular containers of various types and manufacture, including several amphoras.
The objects come from two periods of burial: the first between the late 8th and early 7th century BC, the other between the 7th and early 6th century BC: painted pottery from Corinth, belonging to rather old phases of the protocorinthian production, with refined geometrical decoration, in the older burial areas and to the Ancient Corinthian in the more recent ones: vases of Calcidese colonial production.
Room XXVII. Underwater Archaeology.
Numerous contexts of Eolian underwater archaeology are exhibited. The sea around the islands constitutes an "archaeological gold mine": loads from ships sunk in very dangerous stretches of sea, especially during storms and port tips in landing places now disappeared due to changes in the coastline over the centuries.
The visit begins to the left, moving in a clockwise direction. Amongst the most important exhibits: Ciabatti wreck - Signorini da Pignataro di Fuori, Lipari: it is one of the most ancient loads of the Mediterranean, with pottery from the early Bronze Age (initial phase of the

Capo Graziano culture: early 2nd millennium BC). Pottery fragments from the archaic Greek era to the Renaissance age from the tip of a port, now disappeared, near Monte Rosa on Lipari.
Wreck from the depths near the crag of Dattilo, Panarea: load of black painted pottery possibly made in a Greek city of southern Italy (late 5th - early 4th century BC).
Wreck F from Capo Graziano, Filicudi: Graeco-Italian amphoras and black painted pottery of Eolian production (early 3rd century BC).
Wreck of Secca di Capistello, Lipari: Graeco-Italian amphoras and black painted pottery Campana A (maybe of Neapolitan production, circa 300-280 BC).
Wreck A, Roghi della Secca di Capo Graziano, Filicudi: in the large pyramid in the centre of the room, Wine amphoras Dressel I A and numerous black painted pottery Campana B produced in central Italy. Some Roman bronze coins date the wreck to the 2nd century BC.
Wreck Alberti delle Formiche di Panarea: load of wine amphoras of probable Campana origin and smaller simple vases (amphoras, jugs, etc.). Late 1st century AD.
Wreck of late Roman Imperial Age of Punta Crapazza between Lipari and Vulcano: tin bars of probable Spanish origin, blocks of arsenic sulphide used as colouring etc.
Wreck Filicudi E or 'dei cannoni': three bronze cannons from a Spanish warship of the XVII century.
Climb the stairs to the right of the entrance.

Room XIX.

Reconstruction of the trench from the dig at the late Bronze Age necropolis of Piazza Monfalcone, Lipari (prehistoric Section Room VII).

Room XX.

From this room on all the other rooms of the Classical Pavilion house objects from tombs in the Graeco-Roman necropolis of Contrada Diana, Lipari.
The artefacts on show in room XX offer examples of three categories of product found in the necropolis:

1) Fictile sarcophagi and in lava stone of various typologies (6th-4th century BC).
2) Large vases and amphoras of the Greek era (from 6th to 4th century BC) of various types and manufacture used as containers for objects placed outside the tomb and, sometimes, as cinerary urns.
3) Steles and memorial stones in lava stone of various types which were placed on the tomb as "semata" and in most cases they carried the name of the dead person, from the 5th century BC to the early imperial age. Numerous other steles and memorial stones are kept in the Epigraphic Pavilion.

FIRST FLOOR

Room XXI.

Funeral objects from the 6th, 5th and 4th century BC.
6th century BC (showcase on the right of the entrance and the first two sectors along the East wall). The oldest tombs date back to just after the foundation of the colony of Lipàra (580-576 BC). Among the objects imported pottery, almost all decorated pottery of Corinth, belonging mainly to the very late Corinthian age, particularly the late 6th century BC, which includes a great number of vascular Attic pots (especially from Athens) with much black figured pottery from the last phase of production between 530-525 and 500-490 BC mostly with battle scenes or subjects directly linked to the worship of Dionysus (the God himself, his following of maenads and satyrs etc.), while some fragments of a high standard represent the first phases of the red-figure production between 520 and 490 BC, including the splendid fragment of stamnos probably showing Dionysus, attributed to one of the most important Athenian potters, the so-called Artist of Berlin.
Of particular interest, among other materials, is the presence of an ancient Egyptian statue in light blue *faïence*, a characteristic "ushabti" ("he who responds",

Opposite page : pyramid of wine amphoras in the centre of Room XXVII

Above: objects from a girl's tomb late 5th cent. B.C.

naturally in place of the dead person), important historical evidence of the presence among Lipari's founders of Greeks from the Nile delta.

5th century BC (showcase along the wall to the right of the entrance) still plentiful for the whole century - Attic pottery, both black-painted and red-figured.

Among the latter some large craters used as cinerary urns stand out and are displayed in the first central showcase: two important works of the "manierist" phase between 480 and 465 BC, crater with studs of the Artist "del Porco" with scenes of feasting and of palaestra on the other side; a bell-shaped crater by the "Artist of Providence" Eos (dawn) who chases the boy Tithonos to abduct him, and, on the back, the God Hermes; a small group of craters of the late "classical" style of the late 5th century BC. Few but interesting decorated terracottas: a small group of statuettes from two infant tombs of 470-460 BC shows, over and above the possible symbolic meanings, some pictures of domestic life (a mother bathing a child, a woman sewing, another grinding corn); a large bust of a Goddess (Demetra or Persephone) from the late 5th century BC.

4th century BC. Liparese tomb artefacts offer one of the richest complexes of decorated pottery produced in Greek cities of Sicily.

The beginning of abundant red-figured pottery production, at the end of the century was largely due to strong decline in imports of decorated Attic vases, historically linked to the Peloponnesian war and its western phase (in Sicily).

The cinerary urns displayed in the second, third and fourth central cases belong to a technically and formally more committed production: some of them show figures of clear funerary symbolism, linked to the worship of Dionysus, God of wine but also the God who promises to his devotees, the blessings of the next world, while in others theatre scenes are shown as Dionysus is also God of the theatre.

A first group is composed of craters by "protosicelioti" potters, between the late 5th and mid 4th century BC from the Artists Santapaola to Prado Flenga.

Around 360 BC the craters of the Louvre Group K240, closely linked to the style of the potter Asteas, among which one showing Dionysus watching an acrobatic display and the other with Dionysus intoxicated.

The pictures of mythical episodes are almost all derived from theatrical works: the two goblet craters of the Artist Adrasto, respectively with Adrasto who soothes the dispute between Tideo and Polinice, antecedent to the mythical saga of the Seven at Thebes, with the antecedent of the tragedy "Le Trachinie" by Sophocles (around 350BC); the round goblet crater by the Artist of Syracuse 47099 with Alcmena at the stake from the lost tragedy of Euripides (around 350 BC) with Ulysses in the land of the Cyclops who receives from Maron, priest of Apollo, the leather bag full of wine with which he will intoxicate Polyphemus and with the death of Ippolito, from "Ippolito crowned" by Euripides.

In the window along the north wall of the room are exhibited artefacts of the early 4th century BC (especially the first 25 years): when painted pottery is almost exclusively of Greek-Sicilian production, if not local.

Room XXII.

Artefacts from the 4th century BC (the last 75 years): pottery with red figures is very numerous in this period, especially of

Left: Attic goblet crater of the late 5th cent. B.C.

Above: goblet crater of the Louvre artist, Pan and the Satyrs discover a sleeping maenad, 360 B.C.

Opposite page: masks, characters and statuettes refering to the "comedy" between early 4th cent. B.C. and early 3rd cent. B.C.

Greek-Sicilian production with repetitive icons especially connected with the cultural spheres of Dionysus and Aphrodite.
In particular: vases from the shop of the artist known as Nyn (probably on Lipari between 350 and 325-320 BC), which show clear sytlistic links to the vase painting of workshops from Campania, like the artist Madman, also active on Lipari. Among the most demanding works of the students of the artist Nyn, the large goblet crater with country banqueting scene.
Foremost in Greek-Sicilian red-figured production of the end of the century, was the personality of the Artist of Cefalù, very active in a Lipari workshop. Among his "masterpieces" the lekane (wide cup with cover used as a cosmetics container and other feminine objects) with Apollo and Artemis.
Various objects from the late 4th century are characteri-

sed, especially in the last 25 years, by the presence of Greek-Sicilian pottery with painted decoration (white, yellow and red) of the so-called "Gnathia style" (from the town in Puglia with a flourishing production centre) decorated above all with vine-shoots or convolvulus.
Room. XXIII. Sacred and theatrical terracotta figures. The complex of votive terracottas from the late 4th and early 5th century BC is conspicuous, from the Sanctuary in Contrada Diana dedicated mainly to the worship of the next world: busts and statuettes of Demetra or Kove (Persephone) and of other divinities (Hermes and Artemis), "pinakes" (pictures in relief with priestesses in ritual acts and feminine divinities).
From the necropolis of Lipari a rich and ancient collection of terracottas with theatrical subjects. More than a thousand pieces, models of masks and statuettes, all of local production found on one site: a uniquely interesting opportunity to deepen knowledge of important aspects of the Greek theatre. Their exclusive presence on Lipari, in a funeral context, in tombs and in votive

graves, finds its explanation in the personality of Dionysus, God of the theatre and the God who guarantees blessings in the next life.
Following the order of exhibition: masks from tragedies, satirical dramas (plays with humorous or comic overtones) and ancient comedy (above all caricature of aspects of political and social life of the times); usually associated in the same tomb (as for the statuettes of the Comedy Mezzo) in groups referring to a single play from the first 60 years of the 4th century BC. Several characters from tragedies by Sophocles and Euripides have been identified, some of which have not survived: "Le Tracinie", "Oedipus Rex", and the lost "Filottete at Troy", "The Trojans", "Alcesti", and the lost "Alexandros", "Chrysippos", "Ecuba"; also "Ettore" by Astidamante the younger (tragedy writer of the 4th century BC).
One group of masks should refer to the "Ecclesiazuse" (women in parliament) by Aristophanes (the master of

Ancient Comedy), while the two stupendous masks of Heracles and Hades belong to a lost comedy of a mythological subject. The statuettes of the actors of the comedy "Di Mezzo" are numerous from the late 4th century BC, old and young people, slaves (also negroes), women, with different types of character and behaviour.
Even more numerous is the group of masks (more than 500) of personalities from the New Comedy of Menandro, from a bourgeois environment, whose production began after 290 BC, the year of the writer's death. In the modified theatrical organisation of early Hellenism, the typology appears to be decisively "planned", even though the character of each, with few variants until the Imperial Roman age, is taken with happy expressive realism. 33 of the 44 types listed by Giulio Polluce in his "Onomastikon", encyclopaedia of the 2nd century AD, are represented at Lipari. The types are divided into five categories: old, young, slaves, old women, young women (family women and hetaere).
Finally a group of small fictile reproductions, masks and statuettes, portraits (in bronze and marble) of famous characters Sophocles, Euripides, Menandro, Homer, Socrates, Lisia, Alexander the Great etc.

Room XXIV.

Artefacts from the early 3rd century BC. Until 252-251 BC (destruction of Lipàra by the Romans during the First Punic War).
They are characterised by the abundant presence of decorated pottery in which the traditional red figures are joined by varied lively colours: red, blue, yellow, white etc. which were applied after the firing of the vase, from the Eolian workshops of the early 3rd century BC, which also produced painted pottery in the "Gnathia" style in black paint.
Master of production was the Artist of Lipari, between 300-290 and 270 BC; his students and followers, Artists of the "Sphendone bianca" (a sort of band for women's hair), of the three Nikai (winged victories), of the Dove and the Falcon (whose vase of the same name from Falcone near Tindari is housed in the museum of Palermo) continued his production after the end of his activity.
Also the subjects depicting the female world and reflecting particular aspects of funeral Dionysusism are peculiar: the frequent representation of wedding scenes symbolises the happiness of the mystical union between the soul and the divinity after death.
The artist of Lipari (with the partial exception of the artist of Falcone) is responsible for the major pictorial and compositive works: e.g. the two large "lekanai" with the Beatitudes of the Elysian Fields, the one with the Nereids carrying the arms of Achilles, the two "pissidi skyphoide" (vases with cover - pissidi - in the form of "skyphoi", that is cups with two handles) with the Goddess Hera awaiting marriage etc.
In the field of "Gnathia" style pottery the work of the Artist of the Swans in the decade before the destruction of 252/251 BC is very particular. It is open to a new decorative taste which characterises, in the Greek world, the pottery production of the first Hellenistic phase.
Particularly significant of the phase in which Lipari, from 269 BC, became a Carthaginian naval base , is a funeral stele in lava stone of a Punic type, shaped like an aedicula.
Next to the funeral objects are displayed materials from two "favissae" (votive graves) in the necropolis area.

Room XXV.

Reconstruction of a trench from the dig at the necropolis of Contrada Diana, with tombs of various types, superimposed from the 5th to 3rd century BC.

SECOND FLOOR.

Room XXVI: Lipari - Roman, Byzantine, mediaeval and modern. The visit starts to the left of the entrance. On the western face of the "panel wall" that divides the room is a reconstruction of the external stratigraphy of a tower of the city walls of Contrada Diana with the level

relating to the destruction of 252-251 BC, which gave up stone catapult projectiles and iron weapons along with a coin-safe.

Proceeding to the left, tomb artefacts of Roman times, from the late 3rd century BC to the 2nd century AD. In the Republican Age the artefacts are rather modest, from the late 3rd and 2nd century BC very standardised in their vase typology. Greater variety is offered by the tombs of the late Republican period and the first two centuries of the Imperial age: the two singular vases in terracotta shaped like the head of Iside (with stamp of the potter Dorotheos) and like a dolphin from the same tomb, of around the late 1st century BC, along with singular vases with Egyptian type band decorations; Italic sealed earth, red coral painted pottery (from late 1st century BC to end of 1st century AD); sealed earth of African origin, orange painted pottery (from the late 1st century AD); thin sided vases, especially glasses and small cups with simple decorations (from the 1st century BC to the second century AD); numerous matrix lamps with relief decorated disc of which sufficient examples from the republican period to the late Imperial age are displayed in a special case, glass vases in various forms etc.

Among the other artefacts displayed:

1) Materials of the late 1st and early 2nd century AD from a pottery workshop tip in Contrada Porto delle Genti, Lipari, amphoras for the export of local goods.

2) Two valuable examples of marble sculpture: portrait of a noblewoman from the Flavian Emperors' era (70-90AD) and a Barbarian's head from a sarcophagus with battle scenes between Romans and Barbarians (probably from the early 3rd century AD).

3) Various pagan and Christian funeral epigraphs among which the famous inscription of the Glafiro (2nd century AD) and the Christian inscription of Proba from the late Roman Imperial Age necropolis.

4) Various evidence of the late Roman Imperial and Byzantine age (before the conquest of Lipari by the Arabs in 838): a fragment of altar table, lobate in marble with a relief edge decorated with vine shoots (from Panarea (5th-6th century AD).

Wide range of mediaeval, renaissance and modern pottery from the Castle of Lipari (Cloister of the Norman monastery, wells and sewers) especially of Sicilian, southern Italian and Spanish production.

On display is also a photographic reproduction of "Constitutum" by the Benedictine abbot Ambrogio, an important parchment document (conserved at Patti) of 1095 through which, in Norman times, after the defeat of the Arabs, the repopulation of the islands began.

VULCANOLOGICAL SECTION -Alfredo Rittman.

Opposite the prehistoric pavilion, inside a 15th century house and annex. Education centre - introduction to the geomorphology of the islands (entirely of British production) also important for full understanding of the characteristics of a live volcano. Set out on three floors.

Ground floor: Archaeology and vulcanology.

The natural resources of the islands (obdsidian, pumice, kaolin, sulphur etc. and the various testimonies of their use in relation to cultural material and economic development.

Second floor: General vulcanology.

Third floor: Eolian vulcanology.

SMALL SECTION OF PALEONTOLOGY OF THE QUATERNARY

In a room of the building that housed the infirmary of the Fascist internment camp. On display are fossils from Lipari and other islands, a precious source of knowledge about the morphology and forms of animal and vegetable life during the Quaternary, before the first human settlement.

There are also the remains of the oldest known visitor to the islands: a fragment of a tortoise shell which presumably arrived on a floating trunk or branch enclosed in the piroclastics of Valle Pera, Lipari dating back to between 127000 and 92000 years.

Umberto Spiga
Director of the Eolian Archaeological Museum

Opposite page: "Pisside skyphoide" by the Artist of Lipari - early 3rd cent. B.C.

Above: archaelogical park - Greek sarcophagi found in the Necropolis of contrada Diana

The architecture of the islands, excluding the many archaeological finds, the churches, the castle complex, and the characteristic town houses is made up mainly of rural buildings, designed for agricultural activity, which was once the primary economic activity of the islands.
Very few examples still exist of buildings designed for uses other than dwelling, such as sheds for working or storing pumice stone, some mills, a former hospital, and the spa of San Calogero, now completely rebuilt.
In the period in which the islands were still subject to incursions by the Berber pirates, and until the early 1600s, small watchtowers were built, of which a notable example still stands, almost intact, at Mendolita, along the road which leads to Capistello, standing alone in defence of the store houses and mill side by side. However, the most widespread architecture, with particular characteristics regarding the architectural dimensions and functional and decorative elements, which is recognised as "Eolian architecture," is represented by rural buildings, grouped in small hamlets or isolated in the countryside, mainly used for personal management of agricultural smallholdings.
They are buildings developed according to cellular models, with the placing side by side, or on top of one another, of cube-shaped elements completed with flat roofing in order to better collect rainwater.
Over time other architectural influences, especially from Campania, have become part of the building methods. Rural houses with vertical development are generally made up of two cellular rooms, not inter-communicating inside, but connected by an exterior stairway built on a rampant arch. On the ground floor there was the kitchen, next to which the smaller sheds and services were placed. It was not unusual to have more than one room per floor, and in this case the rooms of the upper floor were connected by a terrace, which was repeated, covered and closed in by large arches, on the floor below.
Horizontal development, however, was more frequent, with a diamond shape, obtained through the placing of successive cellular rooms, not inter-communicating and giving on to a wide terrace, the "bagghiu," generally covered by a pergola on wooden supports, resting on cylindrical pillars, the typical "pulera." Also in this case small outhouses were built alongside the dwelling, and often a wine-vat and stables. The terrace was surrounded by a low wall, in which stone seats called "bisuoli" were made. The floor was covered with tiles of multicoloured majolica and there was a rustic washtub with stone surfaces and, often, the neck of the tank, placed under the "bagghiu," which was designed to collect rainwater.
The "bagghiu," as well as serving to connect the various rooms and storehouses, was the area in which the day to day life of the family took place, under the pergola, which sheltered them from the rays of the sun. Agricultural produce was dried and processed, the family met together in the evening by the light of lanterns (often placed in nooks in the "pulera" to protect the flame from the wind), in short, all the household activities happened there.
Just over the wall of the "bagghiu," there was a small vegetable garden with everyday vegetables, which struggled to grow, watered very little with waste water from the house; in a few rare cases there was a flower bed, full of colours, a luxury considering the scarcity of water.
Next to the house there was an open space, called the "littiera," on which raisins and figs were laid out to dry on characteristic cane mats. These were then put away in the evening, in an open storehouse with a depressed ogive arch, called a "pinnata."
To complete the building, there was sometimes a wine-vat, where grapes were pressed and a threshing yard

Lipari - Mendolita Tower of the 1600s

made of gravel and wrought pozzolanic.
In some larger buildings, a second much larger wood-burning oven was built on the "bagghiu" (one was certainly in the kitchen, next to the hearth, also in stonework covered with tiles), almost exclusively for the cooking of bread, which, once toasted, kept for a long time.
The economy of the islands was poor, so each farm building had to contain everything necessary for day to day survival. The structure of these dwellings was also based on poverty and the need for self-sufficiency. They were made of local stone, of irregular size, cemented with pozzolanic mortar mixed with lime, and the blocks of the roofing were also made of pozzolanic mortar and gravel. It was beaten for a long time with mallets to make it waterproof and was supported with beams made of chestnut and trellis-work.

Above: rural house at Pirera - Lipari

Right: Varesiana ruin - Lipari

The doors and windows had rustic wooden frames, with doors and almost always without glass. They all faced in one direction, towards the "bagghiu," which was on the southern or eastern side of the house, to capture the most sun and the more moderate winds, while the other three sides were rigorously closed.
In some rooms, such as the kitchen, some small holes were made for ventilation; very often old earthenware pans were used to line them precisely.

With agricultural development and the advance of sea transport, the living conditions of the islanders improved and, thanks to more frequent contact with big cities like Naples and Palermo, new influences on the way of life affected even Eolian buildings.
Dwellings became larger, doors and windows were often framed with local stone, the facades were finished off and decorated more carefully, even with curvilinear elements, the crowning walls of the flat roofs were decorated with "lace."
Another decorative element, used above all in the last few centuries, is the finishing off of the house fronts with deep-set patterns in the plaster and bright colours, sometimes in two-colour patterns, with a notable and audacious decorative effect.
This characteristic, which is very evident in these photos of old country houses, has provoked and still provokes a lively debate about the typicality of colouring in Eolian architecture: many local writers, referring to the "white Eolian houses" described in the works of many illustrious visitors (Luigi Salvatore d'Austria, Houel, Vuillier), have maintained that whitewashed houses are typical of Eolian architecture. It is certain that, in periods of serious trouble and fear, because of incursions of Berber pirates, Eolian houses were finished off with local earth mixtures, as camouflage against the background, according to the principle still used in Maghreb countries.
This danger having passed and living conditions having improved, there was certainly a greater care taken in building houses, the painting of which was carried out with lively pigments or natural earth colours, mixed with whitewash, a sign of new wealth and joy shown in the liveliness of the coloured house fronts.

Giuseppe Lo Cascio

Top: Varesiana fresco - Lipari

Bottom: rural house facade Vulcano piano

THE EOLIAN ISLANDS FROM EMIGRATION TO SUSTAINABLE DEVELOPMENT

The Eolian islands, around 1880 experienced a moment of great economic and demographic development. Agriculture and fishing traditionally occupied a large part of the workforce, although the merchant fleets of Lipari, Salina and Stromboli numbered more than 200 ships, with "Paranzieddi", "Bovi", "Marticane" and "Briantini" providing connections with Naples, Livorno, Marseilles and Toulon. It was the success of malmsey which towed along all the other local agricultural products, particularly capers, in demand throughout the Mediterranean.

On Lipari, pumice quarrying began and on Vulcano alum and sulphur excavation was intensified.

A few years later, however, a terrible parasite, phylloxera, destroyed the malvasia vines, the Eolian Mining Company went bust and the inauguration of the railway from Naples to Reggio Calabria took away the Eolians' transport monopoly. The ebbs and flows of history: the economic decline of the islands was repeated, as happened thousands of years before, when the obsidian produced here was replaced by bronze. Emigration to Australia, the USA, Venezuela and Argentina began and , in a few years, decimated the Eolian population. On Panarea the population declined from 1,100 to 300, on Lipari from 12,000 to 8,500, on Salina from 9,000 to 4,000, on Stromboli from 5,000 to 400, on Alicudi from 1,200 to 150 and on Filicudi, which experienced the highest rate of emigration, from 2,500 to 200 inhabitants.

After the Second World War, in a precarious economic climate, agriculture was helped by the construction of water collection basins, to fight against drought and the fishing fleet was increased, becoming the second largest in Sicily.

New work opportunities began to appear for the remaining people, thanks to the arrival of tourists wishing to discover the charm of these wild volcanic islands, which they had seen in popular films (*Stromboli* with Ingrid Bergmand and *Vulcano* with Anna Magnani).

Important archaeological remains were discovered and, thanks to the will of Professor Bernabò Brea and Signora Cavalier, the Eolian Museum was opened, a source of pride for all the islanders, because the underwater artefacts, pottery vases, jewellery and masks bear witness to the importance of the islands in the Mediterranean for thousands of years.

The quarrying of pumice started up again, employing more than 200 people by the 1970's. Tourism contributed to economic improvement; the first hotels and restaurants were opened and houses were restored to be rented out in summer. Italian tourists purchased land and houses abandoned by emigrants, often at bargain prices, doing them up as summer homes. In the 70's and 80's despite considerable financial resources, sometimes a result of patronage, there was a stagnation of planning and public works. Everybody was contented with the positive economic trend and hoped it would continue.

Now the reductions in public spending have created serious economic imbalance. Concern about the present economic situation is accompanied by new plans and efforts to ensure development of the islands.

For example, the adoption of a "rural plan" as a means of territorial planning; the development of new opportunities with investment in "sea farming" (the breeding of marine species in tanks in the sea) and the organising of training courses on Lipari, for "sea farming" plant technicians, to start young people up in this new type of work; plans for other courses in the port service sector, presented to the Region for funding, in anticipation of the "Ports Plan". These are some of the measures adopted by the present administration.

In agriculture, with EU resources, plans have been made to relaunch typical products, such as malmsey, capers and raisins, and to create a service centre for tourism in the small Sicilian islands. There is an intention to open the first experimental wine cellar in the Eolian islands and to increase tourism, through interest in nature, culture and spas.

The Eolian islands have begun to receive a new image with the cultural festival "Constitutum", which is the celebration of the 900th anniversary of the birth of the "Communitas Eoliana", and which has received national and international attention.

We invest today, thinking of tomorrow, to make our islands more hospitable, to improve living conditions, to create development, so that nobody will be forced to leave their homeland.

Luigi Amato

If Eolian cuisine is so inspired, changeable, variegated, so full of unifying and contrasting moods at the same time, it is also thanks to the incredible concentration of history, culture, and customs that have gradually followed one another. In every dish there is ancient wisdom which the Eolian islanders have managed to enrich, elaborate and transform, until they make it an original and unrepeatable gastronomic experience.
The principal characteristic of Eolian cuisine is the constant and wise use of fragrant herbs which fill every dish with scent, hidden sensations, shadowy moods: rosemary, oregano, basil, garlic, "nepitella", mint along with summer lemon peel, tomatoes "a pennula" and, obviously, capers. Fish is central to every meal, simply grilled and seasoned with a little oil and a drop of lemon or stuffed with tomato, basil, garlic, capers and a little soaked bread crumb. Of equal importance are squid and lobster.
Cakes are also symbols of holidays: at carnival time the "gigi", for Saint Joseph's Day the "vastidduzze" with raisins and almonds, for Christmas the "spicchitedi" of mulled wine.
Finally, lemon liqueur and malmsey, "nectar of the Gods", before and after meals, along with sesame biscuits.
The recipes below are not only from traditional cuisine, and nor could they be, because of the history of the island and their repopulation and the development of recent years, which has influenced culinary customs.
They are a mixture of typical cuisine and revised cuisine, but with respect for tradition.

Salad with oranges, lemons, smoked swordfish and capers

Ingredients for 4 people:

8 slices of smoked swordfish "à la julienne"
1 large juicy orange (cut into segments without pith)
1 large ripe lemon (cut into segments without pith)
7 tablespoons of extra-virgin olive oil
2 tablespoons of capers

2 tablespoons of white vinegar
1 tuft of chopped basil and mint
12 peeled almonds "à la julienne"
Paprika and salt as needed

Put together all the ingredients and mix them for a few minutes with the dressing made with the oil, capers, vinegar, herbs and almonds, adding salt and pepper.
Serve cool.

Recipe of the restaurant "Filippino"

Spaghetti with tomatoes "a pennula"

A very simple pasta dish whose particular taste comes from the very small round tomatoes, typical of the Eolian islands, which the locals "hang up" in large conical baskets, so they can be eaten in winter too.

Ingredients: only tomato "a scocca" or "pennula", typical of the Eolian islands must be used; extra-virgin olive oil, basil and garlic, just a pinch of oregano and paprika.

In a large frying pan, fry a generous helping of garlic (which is then taken out) and a good bit of paprika. Then put in the tomatoes, cut in half, with their skins but without pips, and let them dry out on a high flame with a little salt and oregano. After draining the spaghetti mix it in the frying pan and generously sprinkle freshly chopped basil. If you like you can add grated ricotta.

Taken from "Cucina Eoliana"
Pungitopo Editions

Scorpion Fish a ghiotta alla Liparota

This is a traditional Mediterranean recipe, but the Eolian scorpion fish are without equals for taste.

Ingredients for 4 people:

2 Scorpion fish of 500 grams each
3 small onions
3 ripe tomatoes
8 green olives
1 spoonful of capers
1 tuft of parsley
basil leaves
1\2 glass of dry white wine
3 tablespoons of olive oil
toasted bread, pepper and salt.

Preparation and cooking time:
45 minutes.

Gut the scorpion fish, cut off all the prickly fins, scale them, wash them in running water and leave them to drip.
Clean the onions and slice them finely; wash the tomatoes, remove the skins and seeds and cut them into small cubes; remove the stones from the olives, wash and finely chop the basil and parsley.
Heat the olive oil in a pan, brown the onions, add the olives and tomatoes and cook for 1-2 minutes.
Add the scorpion fish, the capers and the chopped herbs. Pour in the white wine and a glass of water and cook in the covered pan for about 30 minutes.
10 minutes before the end of cooking, add salt and pepper as desired and end the cooking by removing the lid.
Serve with croutons of toasted bread.

Recipe of the restaurant "Filippino"

Stuffed Totani (Squid)

Every Eolian islander worth his salt goes fishing for "totani" one night a month. Even when there is no other fish on the island, "totani" can be found. the "totano" is a fat and tough type of squid, with a "wild" taste, and much appreciated by gourmets. Cooking in sauces and stewing is best for this fish. The filling suggested here is very simple, typically Eolian and exalts the prince of fishes of these islands. You can vary it according to your taste, mood and desire to amaze your guests.

Ingredients:

one large "totano" per person

tomato sauce

parsley, plenty of mint

garlic, desalinised capers, bread crumbs

two eggs, black pepper, green olives.

Clean the totani, cutting off the tentacles and leaving the hood whole to be filled. Cook the tentacles in oil. Add salt and a little wine and cook on a low flame for a while. Take the fish out of the pan and, on a low flame, with more oil, fry two cloves of crushed garlic. Then add the tomato sauce, the chopped parsley, and a little salt. Let the sauce cook a little. In the meantime prepare the stuffing with two beaten eggs, bread crumbs, the olives cut into pieces, the black pepper, the chopped capers and the tentacles. Fill the fish, close it with toothpicks or, better still, with a needle and thread and cook it as long as necessary in the tomato sauce.
It can also be cooked in the oven in a baking-pan with oil and a little white wine. In this case, it is advisable not to use eggs in the stuffing, but to add more mint, basil and some desalinised anchovies. Some advice: to make them softer, before stuffing them fry them for a moment to dry them out and make them lose all their water.
Another way of stuffing them is to prepare the filling with the tentacles, egg, parsley, pieces of melted cheese, bread crumbs, grated parmesan, peas, celery and carrots cut into small pieces. An original stuffing - the fish should be cooked in a frying -pan, over a low heat, with a chopped onion in the oil, a drop of white wine, a leaf of laurel and a thin strip of fish.

Taken from "Cucina Eoliana"
Pungitopo Editions.

Gigi

A typical Eolian sweet made during carnival.

Ingredients for six people:

Flour 500g.

Lard 100g.

Two egg yolks

Sugar 75g.

Half a glass of white wine

A glass of mulled wine

Mix the flour, lard, egg yolks and sugar until you obtain a soft, smooth mixture. Leave the mixture to settle for about 15 minutes, then roll it out in thin sticks and cut these into pieces of a centimetre each.
Then take a deep frying-pan and put it on a high flame gradually putting the pieces of mixture into deep oil, turning them from time to time, until they turn golden.
After frying all the pieces dip them in a small pan of warm mulled wine, turn them twice and then lay them out on an oval plate dusting them with sugar.

Recipe of the restaurant "Filippino".

Until 1930 the whole island was covered with pathways for the farmers to reach the fields and the pumice workers to reach the quarries. Then the abandonment of the land to emigrate, or work in the tourist industry, led to their partial loss under thick vegetation. Broom, heather, oleander, rosemary and myrtle colour and scent the island. Walking unhurriedly through untouched and wild countryside is probably the best experience the island can offer.
The island has a good network of public transport and the friendly drivers will stop wherever you want. The terminus is at Marina Lunga at the end of Corso Vittorio Emanuele, but the buses also stop at Marina Corta. If you prefer a bike or a moped you can contact **Roberto Foti** (Tel. 9812352), **Marcello** (Tel. 9811234) or **Giuseppe Cannizzaro** (Tel. 9811408) or for a car the **Basile** brothers (Tel. 9811781), **Mega Service** (Tel. 9812989) or the **Tony taxi service** (Tel. 0338-8110546).
For hiking you need information on the old pathways. The Tourist Information Office (Tel. 9880095), on the Corso, or the excellent excursion guide to the islands can provide this.
Heading south, after San Nicola, you turn right at the first junction and climb up. Turning right again towards San Salvatore, we find an old naval watchtower, used as a **geographical observatory** today. From the little square where the paved road ends there is a spectacular view: the island of Vulcano, with Vulcanello and its crater and cone and the isthmus. Climbing up some steps and following a path of about 200 metres you reach the viewing point of **Falcone.**

On foot, using a pathway which leaves from San Nicola, or by road passing above San Bartolo, you can reach **Monte Guardia** (369 metres high). Following the western side of the mountain, a track on the right leads to a lava spike. In front of you there are the sheer cliffs down to the sea, Perciato point, the crags (Pietra Lunga and Pietra Monalda) and, in the background, Vulcano: a delightful view.
It is possible to make a tour of the island in a day but, given the number of interesting places to visit, it is better to plan a number of

Above: Chiesa dell'Annunziata

Left: Spa of S. Calogero

excursions.
In your own car or by bus you can head for the mountainous part of the island. Following the winding road which leads to **Pianoconte**, on the right after 4 km, you find the **church of the Annunziata** with its particular staircase. A little further on there is **Quattrocchi**, with its lovely view of the crags and smoking Vulcano. Before the village of Pianoconte, with a short diversion of two kilometres to the left, you reach **the spa of San Calogero**. The present building was constructed in 1867 and recently restored, but is not yet in use. The waters have always been used to cure gout and rheumatism. Nearby, as proof of the spa tradition, there are two Graeco-Roman baths and one from the 1800s. Recent digs have revealed a Roman spa pool of the second century AD and a Mycenaean **"tholos"** 3,500 years old. It is a building with a circular cupola, in igloo shape, built in imitation of Mycenaean princely tombs and used, in Roman times, as a thermal sauna, with water at 60°C from a nearby source and with a bath and circular stone seat inside. From the spa, following some pathways, you can reach Monte **Mazzacaruso**, so-called because the Greeks used to throw malformed babies from the top. From here you can see in the distance the twin mounts of Salina and also Filicudi and Alicudi. Going back towards **Pianoconte**, it is possible to stop off for lunch in the nearby restaurants: A **Menza** **Quartara, La Ginestra** and **Le Macine** and if you reach **Quattropani**, after five kilometres of fields and vineyards, the restaurant "**A Cannata**." At Pianoconte every year in November **the bread and wine festival** takes place, celebrating the life of the farmers: the milling of grain, bread-making, the manufacture of wool, the pressing of grapes. Games, a photographic exhibition, a sausage barbecue and a dance in the square complete the day. Quattropani is a small group of houses scattered across a plateau. From here it is worth making a diversion to the right, at the cemetery, to go to the **Santuario della Madonna della Catena**, a little white Greek-style country church of the 17th century, recently resto-

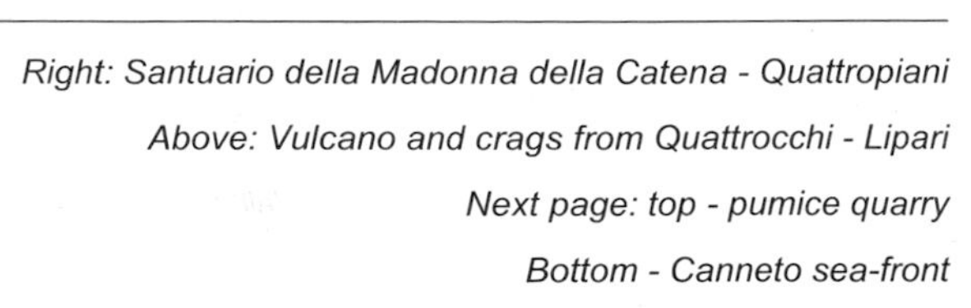

Right: Santuario della Madonna della Catena - Quattropiani

Above: Vulcano and crags from Quattrocchi - Lipari

Next page: top - pumice quarry

Bottom - Canneto sea-front

red. It is called Chiesa Vecchia to distinguish it from the one built along the road by the houses. From the Sanctuary you can see Salina with its lighthouse and the village of Lingua. Going down the side of **Monte Chirica**, you return to sea level and the temperature changes. You pass by **Acquacalda** and its beach on the long quay, used by the ships to load pumice. Here we are at the base of one of the two pumice quarrying zones, where eruptions have created steep white gorges.
After the wide curve of **Punta Castagna**, you arrive at the beach of **Porticello** and the other vast area of pumice quarries, called **Campo Bianco**. We are at the foot of **Monte Pelato**, which in 727 formed a flow of obsidian called Rocche Rosse because of its ochre and brown colouring. More quays follow in a surreal white environment with the sea which stands out blue. Further on, at **Punta Sparanello**, you can make a diversion to **Lami** and observe an impressive flow of obsidian. It is the flow which provided raw materials in the eneolithic period, making Lipari a centre of trade. In this area there are the greatest number of extinct volcanoes covered with vegetation. We then arrive at the long village of **Canneto**, originally born to house those who worked pumice, and later becoming the second village of the island. Along the lovely beach, very full in summer, a lot of fishing boats are pulled out of the sea. There is no lack of restaurants and bars and the-

re is a disco. The last diversion we advise is towards **Pirrera**, at the end of the village of Canneto. Arriving in the place after 2 km, you can continue on foot to the summit of the **Forgia Vecchia**. You can then return to the coast and, through a tunnel under **Monte Rosa**, you get back to Lipari after passing **Marina Lunga**.

DISCOVERING THE SEA

About ten buses a day connect Lipari to the **beaches** of **Canneto, Papesca, Porticello and Acquacalda**, without the need to hire a boat to get there. However to discover the sea, with its sheltered coves, crags and beaches inaccessible by land, a boat is essential. To **hire a boat**, with or without a guide, at Canneto you can contact: **Roberto Foti** (tel. 9880825), **Franco La Greca, Nautic Centre** (tel. 9812725), **Evelyn Speglic, Eolmare Calandra** (tel. 9880147) and **Daniela Manni** (tel. 9811538); at Marina Corta "**Gli amici della costa**" (tel. 9822148), **the Centro Nautico Eoliano, Eolian Holidays** (tel. 9880456), **Mega Service** (tel. 9812989), **Da Maurizio** (tel. 9822040) and **Roberto Foti** (tel. 9812352); then at **Porto delle Genti, Basile e Cappadona** (tel. 9880486), at **Valle Muria, Anna Maria Famigletti** (tel. 0360-289141) and, at Marina Lunga, **Natoli** (tel. 9886156).

It is possible to go on organised **trips** around Lipari, or other islands, on ships which also serve lunch on board: **Viching** (tel. 0330-695886), **Pignataro Shipping** (tel. 0368-675975), **Motoveliero Sigismond** (tel. 9812852), Sen (tel. 9812341) and **Nauta Yacht Broker** to rent yachts from 9 to 20 metres (tel. 9822305).
From Marina Corta we move southwards making a tour of the island clockwise. We move past the flat areas which give way to high jagged hilltops. Rounding **Punta Crapazza**, we find the beach of **Vinci**, where you can swim with a view of the **crags and Vulcano**. This is the nearest point to Vulcano and once Lipari and Vulcano were, perhaps, one island. We continue towards the imposing crags, **Pietra Lunga** and **Pietra Menalda**. This area is excellent for divers. According to some, these immense cliffs are the "**Planktai Petrai**" referred to by Circe to Ulysses returning home: "You will see high cliffs dropping sheer into the sea, battered thunderingly by the surge of Amphytryon, no ship ever escaped from here, the breakers sweep away only the wrecks of ships and bodies of men. Only one ship managed to pass by, the famous Argo." The reference is to the arch that the sea has created in the crag of Pietra Lunga which commands awe. Near the coast the **Brigghio** sticks up, as high as an obelisk. The lava promontory of **Punta del Perciato** forms an arch of lava through which a boat can pass. Opposite the Perciato

there are some small cliffs, called **Le Formiche**, with a shallow bottom, suitable for diving. We pass by high cliffs, under the mountain, and rounding **Punta di Levante**, we reach the **beach of Valle Muria**. A beautiful shingle beach for a pleasant stop. Larger boats find good shelter here from the winds and a suitable anchorage. Further on is **Pietra del Bagno**, with a stretch of coast in which there are several caves. Among small coves we meet **Cala Fico, Punta del Cugno Lungo and Punta Palmeto**. It is perhaps the most beautiful stretch of coastline, with little islands, caves, sheer copper-coloured cliffs, with the mountain standing above. There is a little sheltered beach behind **La Scarpa** cliff.....a secret for any readers in search of quiet spots. From here you can visit the nearby **Grotta del Palmeto** and the **Torricelle**, big magnificent crags. After the stretch of "**sulphured**" coast, and after rounding **Punta del Legno Nero**, the coast becomes less steep and we meet **Acquacalda** and the pumice quarry, which stands out from far off, with the quay sticking out into the sea. Further on we reach **Punta della Castagna**, with a beach at the foot of the high pumice walls. The white deposits accompany us for a long while, with quays once used for transporting pumice, and with a white sea bed and turquoise water because of the sediments. High up you notice the flow of obsidian of the Rocche Rosse. Passing the **Campo Bianco** and the beach of **Papesca**, we arrive at **Canneto**.

Rounding Monte Rosa, an ancient volcano on which we advise a trip, we arrive at **Porto Pignataro** with fishing boats and yachts moored there. We follow the coast of **Marina Lunga** and finally we are welcomed by **the Castle Rock**.

You can organise diving courses and cruises in the islands by contacting **Enrico Lo Mazzi** (tel. 9880088) and **Kurt Wahlen** (tel. 9812060), **Andi's Dive Centre** (tel. 9822238), **Centro Nautico Eoliano** (tel. 9812437), **Diving Centre Mantra** Club (tel. 9811004) and the **Sud-Est Diving Centre** (tel. 9812510). For refilling tanks just contact the same people.

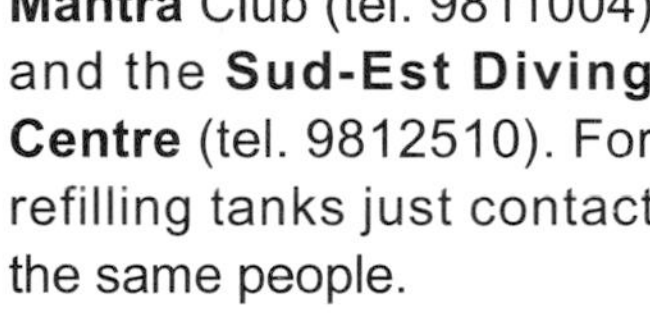

WHERE AND WHAT TO EAT

A glass of malmsey is very good as an aperitif, before deciding where to dine. There are many restaurants and trattorie of a good standard. Here are some suggestions.

Left: Campobianco on the slopes of Monte Pelato

Above: Pietra del Bagno

Opposite page: top - Pietra Lunga crag

Bottom - Punta del Peccato

IN THE CENTRE

- FILIPPINO - The best known restaurant on Lipari, in piazza Mazzini, founded in 1910. It has a large tank with lobsters. Among the many recipes worth remembering are the raviolini with grouper, fish carpaccio, scorpion fish "a ghiotta."
- E PULERA - In via Diana, under a pergola in a beautiful flowering garden. Particularly good are the velette all'eoliana, the roulades of swordfish and a salad of oranges, lemons, smoked swordfish and capers.
- LA NASSA - Mentioned in many restaurant guides, it offers typical Eolian cuisine: coachman's treble and roulades of imperial louvar.
- LA PIAZZETTA - In piazza Monfalcone, it serves maccheroni alla piazzetta, squid "ca muddica" and swordfish alla liparota.
- TRATTORIA D'ORO - Comfortable place to eat with a fish based menu. Swordfish ravioli and seafood skewers.
- TRATTORIA DEL VINCOLO - Home cooking such as penne alla liparota and grilled squid. Recommended the caponata.
- IL GALEONE - Restaurant and pizzeria serving rigatoni alla Galeone and grilled fish.
- BARON DES CHEFS - Among its specialities pappardelle au gratin with basil and swordfish steak with green pepper.
- RITROVO SOTTOMONASTERO - Restaurant and pizzeria, offering Eolian hors d'oeuvres, home-made pasta and swordfish roulades.

- BLUE MOON - Restaurant and pizzeria in piazza Mazzini.
- DAL PESCECANE - Spaghetti with clams and escalopes alla isole eolie.
- LA MUNCIARDA - Simple and genuine cuisine offering maccheroni allo joncu.

MARINA CORTA

- DA BARTOLO - Maccheroni alla Bartolo with chopped spicy pesto, barbecued fish or fish with onions.
- AL PIRATA - Pizzeria and restaurant which offers taglioli-ni allo scoglio and grouper roulades with chicory.
- A SFIZIUSA - Recommended are the spaghetti alla sfiziusa with capers, olives and parsley, pesto alla sfiziusa and stuffed squid.
- FRATELLI SALANITRO MARE
- NENZYNA - Home cooking, risotto alla pescatore and fish soup.
- DAL NAPOLETANO - Genuine cooking, seafood and grilled fish.

TOWARDS PORTINENTE

- CARASCO HOTEL - Eolian and international cuisine. The chef advises linguine with scorpion fish sauce and roulades of imperial louvar. Wide choice of wines.
- GROTTA DEL SARACENO - Looking over the Bay of Porto delle Genti, with its elegant terraces, in a splendid garden. Fettuccine del Saraceno and swordfish. Excellent pizzas.
- HOTEL GIARDINO SUL MARE - A terrace overlooking the sea in a blooming garden. Pasta alla melanciova with fried aubergines, anchovies and parsley, baked maigre and impeccable service.

At Marina Lunga there is the restaurant STELLA DEL MARE which offers pasta alla stella del mare, fish soup and Sicilian cassata.

Above Pignataro, from the terraces of the Pinnata, you enjoy a wonderful view of the harbour of Lipari while tasting the chef's specialities.

We also recommend the RITROVO LA LANTERNA, for sandwiches, snacks and beer and MOBY DICK, a snack bar and ice-cream parlour, open till late.

CANNETO

- RITROVO CALANDRA - To have a pizza, spaghetti cirucco and swordfish roulades.
- RITROVO MIRAMARE.

We also remind you of il Mocambo, l'Odissea, il Piccolo Bar, Papisca and Sol et Maris.

ACQUACALDA

- DA LAURO.
- TRE ARCHI - Eolian pasta with capers and tomato. Stuffed squid.

QUATTROPANI

- A MENZA QUARTARA - In the countryside, its specialities are "pasta di ziti" and sweet and sour rabbit. "La Bouche" is a pizza known throughout the islands.

PIANOCONTE

- LA GINESTRA - Typical Eolian cuisine, the original black tagliatelle alla matriciana di mare, scorpion fish "a ghiotta", squid alla eoliana and sweet and sour rabbit. Variety of wines and liqueurs.
- LE MACINE - Restaurant and pizzeria with a very varied menu. Among the many dishes on offer are the tagliolini in salsa paesana, the controfiletto with garden herbs and home-made cakes and rosolio.

WHERE TO STAY

HOTELS

- HOTEL VILLA MELIGUNIS ♥♥♥♥ An elegant 18th century villa, restored in Mediterranean style with a view over Marina Corta and the Castle (tel. 9812246).
- HOTEL CARASCO ♥♥♥ Dominating the cove of Porto delle Genti, it is in a beautiful position. Swimming pool and road down to the sea (tel. 9811605).
- GATTOPARDO PARK HOTEL ♥♥♥ Located in a 19th century villa and Eolian style houses in a garden of palm trees and bougainvillaea (tel. 9811035).
- GIARDINO SUL MARE ♥♥♥ Built on an outcrop of rock overlooking the bay of Lipari, as its name suggests, it is characterised by a lovely garden. Swimming pool and road down to the sea (tel. 9811004).
- ROCCE AZZURRE ♥♥♥ Facing Porto delle Genti, it was the first hotel to be built on Lipari. Good service (tel. 9811582).
- HOTEL VILLA AUGUSTUS ♥♥ Right in the centre, it is an oasis of peace among scented flowers (tel. 9811232).
- LA FILADELFIA ♥♥ In the centre, near the Diana archaeological park, with a large garden. Apartments are also available (tel. 9812485).
- HOTEL ORIENTE ♥♥ In contrada Diana, near the archaeological park, various archaeological artefacts have been found in its lovely garden. There is an interesting collection of objects regarding arts and crafts (tel. 9811493)
- MOCAMBO ♥♥ Hotel and restaurant on Canneto Bay (tel. 9811442).
- NERI ♥♥ Quiet family-run guest house. Liberty style building (tel. 9811413).
- ODISSEA ♥♥ Hotel and restaurant near the sea, at Canneto.
- HOTEL POSEIDON ♥♥ Open all year. Very near the port with a garden.
- VILLA DIANA ♥♥ Family-run guest house in contrada Diana. Wide terraces and quiet gardens, period furniture.

EUROPEO ♥ A hotel on the main street.

LOCANDA SALINA♥ At the foot of the Castle Rock.

ROOMS FOR RENT

- ENZO IL NEGRO - In via Garibaldi, near Marina Corta: clean and cheap (tel. 9813163).
- LAURICELLA ROSA - At Marina Lunga, an Eolian style house near the sea.

We also recommend, Giuseppe Scoglio (tel. 9811358), Diana Brown (tel. 9812584), Tullio Cammarano (tel. 9812386), Vittorio Casa (tel. 9811523), Francesco De Gregorio (tel. 9811866), Maria Lo Nardo (tel. 9812054), Maria Pia Martello (tel. 9811634), Concetta Muleta (tel. 9811339), Ignazia Princiotto (tel. 9812614), Tommaso Profilo (tel. 9812896), Bartolo Tomarchio (tel. 9811423) and Barbara Villa (tel. 9811695).

FURNISHED APARTMENTS

La Villetta residence (tel. 9813000), Residence La Giara (tel. 9880352), Residence Mendolita (tel. 9811002), Mariangela rent (tel. 9886017), Costa Residence Vacanze (tel. 9880740), Residence Fiorentino (tel. 9880573), Residence Regione (tel. 9812012), Francesco De Gregorio (tel. 9811866), Antonio Puglisi (tel. 9811492), Armando Riitano (tel. 0360-864044).

TRAVEL AGENCY

Eolioan Tours (tel. 9812193), Menalda Tours (tel. 9813131), Ossidiana Travel (tel. 9811519), Costa Meligunte Travel (tel. 9880740), Longo Travel (tel. 9880640).

ESTATE AGENCY

Eolian Holidays (tel. 9880456), Eoliana Immobiliare (tel. 9813243), House Service (tel. 9813169), Natoli's Agency (tel. 9811964), Orso Bruno (tel. 9812012), Ruden (tel. 9811255).

AFTER DINNER

At night the island comes alive even more because, after a day of sun and sea, everybody crowds into the Corso and Marina Corta. People meet here to decide where to spend the evening. There are numerous possibilities. We recommend the Kasbah Cafè, in via Maurolico, a pretty garden where there is live music, the Chitarra Bar at Marina Corta, and the Cerchio di Bacco, in via Capistello, with its concerts and excellent meals. There are three discos on the island: il Turmalin in piazza Municipio with various DJs and dancing "under the stars"; La Pinnata above the port of Pignataro, at the end of Marina Lunga; La Calandra at Canneto.

SAINT BARTHOLOMEW: THE SAINT FROM THE EAST

"The story of his passion says that Bartholomew Apostle was martyred in Asia. Many years after his passion, during a new wave of persecution against Christians, the pagans saw the people praying at his tomb and, out of hate, took away his body, placed it in a lead sarcophagus and threw it into the sea saying: may you never have influence over out people again. But with the intervention of God's Providence the lead sarcophagus, carried away by the waters, was transported to an island called Lipari. This was revealed to the Christians so they could collect it: the body was collected and buried and a great temple was built around it. It is now invoked and shows its benefit to many people with its virtues and graces."

In this way, around 580 AD, Saint Gregory of Tours wrote in his "Libri Miraculorum".

There was, then, on Lipari - already in the 6th century - a tradition about the arrival of the sacred body: a great temple was put up in honour of the Protector; and there was also a movement of foreign pilgrims who came to test the "virtues" and "graces" of those thaumaturgic remains, but to say that devotion to St. Bartholomew and this form of primitive tourism date back to 264, as local tradition would have it, would perhaps be rash. However, it remains a certain fact things on Lipari were like this for a long time before the ancient French writer mentioned them, so let's consider the reasons. Between 200 and 250 AD there was a crisis in Rome of all sectors of economic and political life, and of most of the ancient civil and institututional values of the Empire. The peoples of the provinces demonstrated their desire to govern themselves.

In this atmosphere, full of political and social ferment, Christianity made its first giant and triumphant leap forward in the pagan world and, in particular, in Sicily and along the Tyrrhenian coast of Italy.

At this point the Emperor Decio, in 249, started a general persecution, which continued under his successor, Valeriano, until 258. Christians held responsible for such ill-fated social transformation were to be eliminated, and the number of victims is incalculable. At that time the gesture of martyrdom began to be exalted among Christians, as did the personality of the martyrs, those who had shown their faith to Christ by giving their own life.

The martyrs were called "saint" and people were convinced that the Holy Martyrs, on judgment day, would be the first to be awakened and admitted to the beatific vision without having to undergo the anxiety of God's judgement.

To attenuate the apocalyptic fears of the "finis mundi" and "dies judici" the Christians gave a new dimension to the personality of the martyrs. The idea of being able to guarantee the help of a Holy Martyr was a great consolation to everybody; finding him next to you on Resurrection Day would certainly constitute a pass for eternity. Consequently, there was a rush to obtain

Left: Lipari, 17th cent. chapel of St. Bartholomew

Opposite page top: statue of St. Bartholomew

Opposite page bottom: Lipari, Cathedral altar

suitable burial places for the martyrs in public and private cemeteries, even at very great expense. But it was worth it: when the angels' trumpets blew, the Martyr would ascend to heaven, dragging a host of his devout admirers. Since not everybody had a Martyr at his private disposition, an alternative belief grew up: a single martyr, though officially Protector of the Christians in a certain area, would have the same powers to the advantage of the whole collectivity.
The Christian community of Lipari was on of the first, in the West, to open up to worship of the Martyrs, to demand a Protector for itself and assure itself of the physical presence, through appropriation, of his mortal remains. The Liparèi had no local martyrs to honour and so fell back on one of the Apostles of Jesus. An apostle was considered martyr for having been a direct witness of the Lord's works and for having made, in His name, the extreme sacrifice.
The preference of the Liparèi could only fall on St. Bartholomew who must have exercised such an exceptionally fruitful and adventurous activity and, moreover, had suffered such an inhuman and complex death that, in the end, nobody knew where he had preached and how he had been martyred. Was he beheaded? Was he burnt at the stake? Was he skinned alive? Only one thing is sure: the dedication of St. Bartholomew to the service of the Lord provoked great admiration among the faithful. Perhaps the Liparèi of that time, almost all men of the sea, were attracted by the name, a name which in Aramaic was Nathanael Bar-Tholmaì, Gift of God, son of he who moves the waters.
He must also have the power to dominate the blind forces of nature. Regarding the acquisition of the holy body, it is to be believed that a foreign crew, passing through Lipari, gave, in return for money, a mummified body claimed to be that of the great Apostle, or that sailors from Lipari, stopping in far-off ports were tempted to buy it in good faith.
As you can see, we are talking of events in a past which is too distant and obscure for us to be able to judge the authenticity of those remains. After all in the second half of the 3rd century there were numerous requests for saints' bodies; profiteers readily offered skeletons or bones claimed to be of Apostles, Evangelists or martyrs. Time and the fallibility of man's memory did the rest and, on the blank page of history our vivid imagination gradually created and recorded miracles (the floating stone coffin, the difficulty of pulling it out of the water). The Liparèi of the 6th century had a nasty surprise: some writers maintained that the holy body lay at Dàrae, in Mesopotamia, and others in Phrygia.
But the people of Lipari remained faithful to the memory of their Protector then and also in 838, when his remains were removed to Benevento and their dismay was replaced by the belief that there were still excellent reasons why he should remain their Protector, ready to block God's punishment in case of earthquakes, famine and plagues.

Taken from G. IACOLINO,
"Gente delle Eolie"
Publisher Aldo Natoli,
Lipari 1994, pg. 108-113

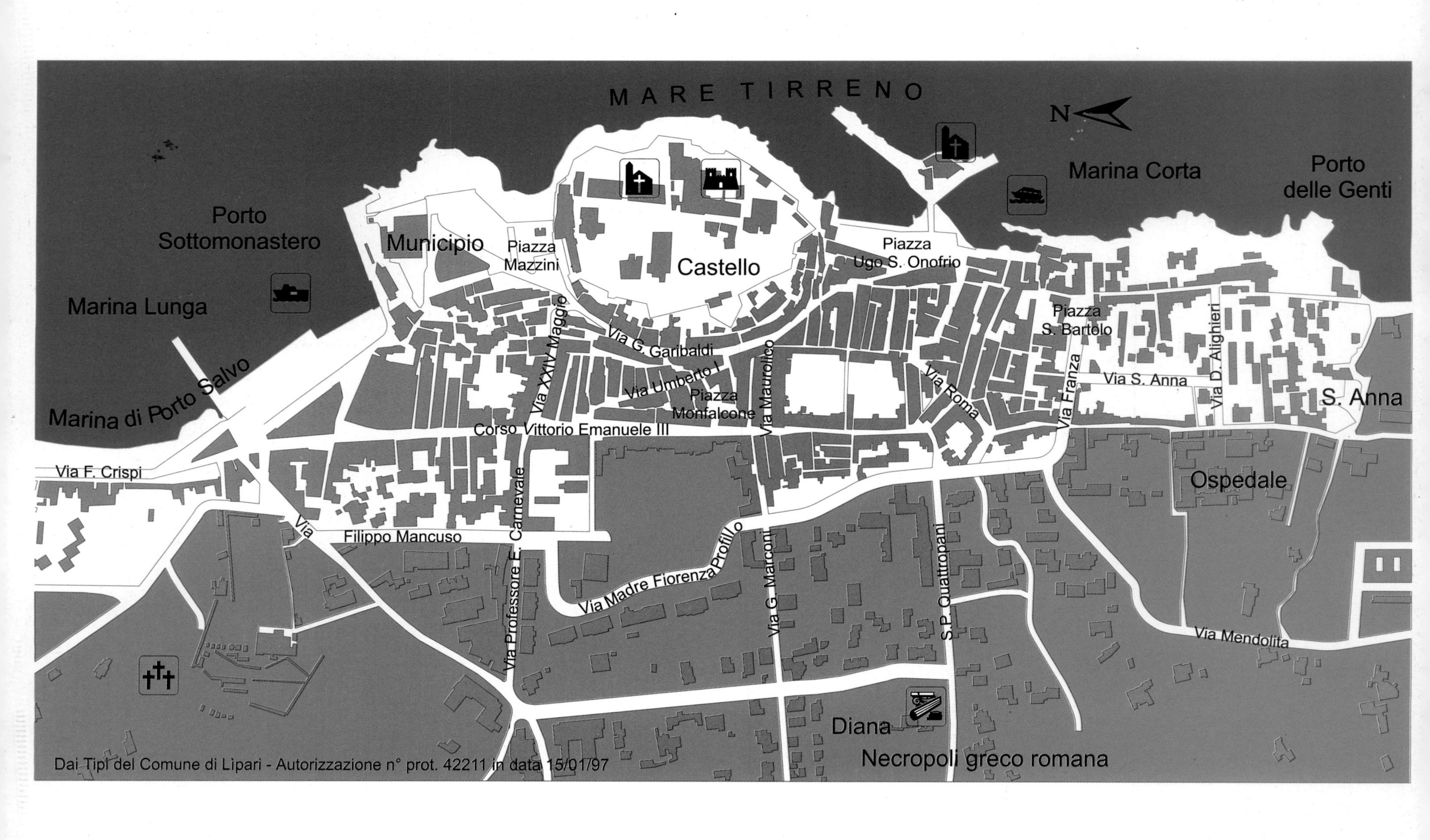
MARE TIRRENO
N
Marina Corta
Porto
delle Genti
Porto
Sottomonastero
Municipio
Piazza
Mazzini
Castello
Piazza
Ugo S. Onofrio
Marina Lunga
Marina di Porto Salvo
Piazza
S. Bartolo
Via D. Alighieri
Via S. Anna
S. Anna
Via G. Garibaldi
Via XXIV Maggio
Via Umberto I
Piazza
Monfalcone
Via Maurolico
Via Roma
Via Franza
Corso Vittorio Emanuele III
Via F. Crispi
Ospedale
Via Filippo Mancuso
Via Professore E. Carnevale
Via Madre Fiorenza Profilio
Via G. Marconi
S.P. Quattropani
Via Mendolita
Diana
Necropoli greco romana
Dai Tipi del Comune di Lipari - Autorizzazione n° prot. 42211 in data 15/01/97

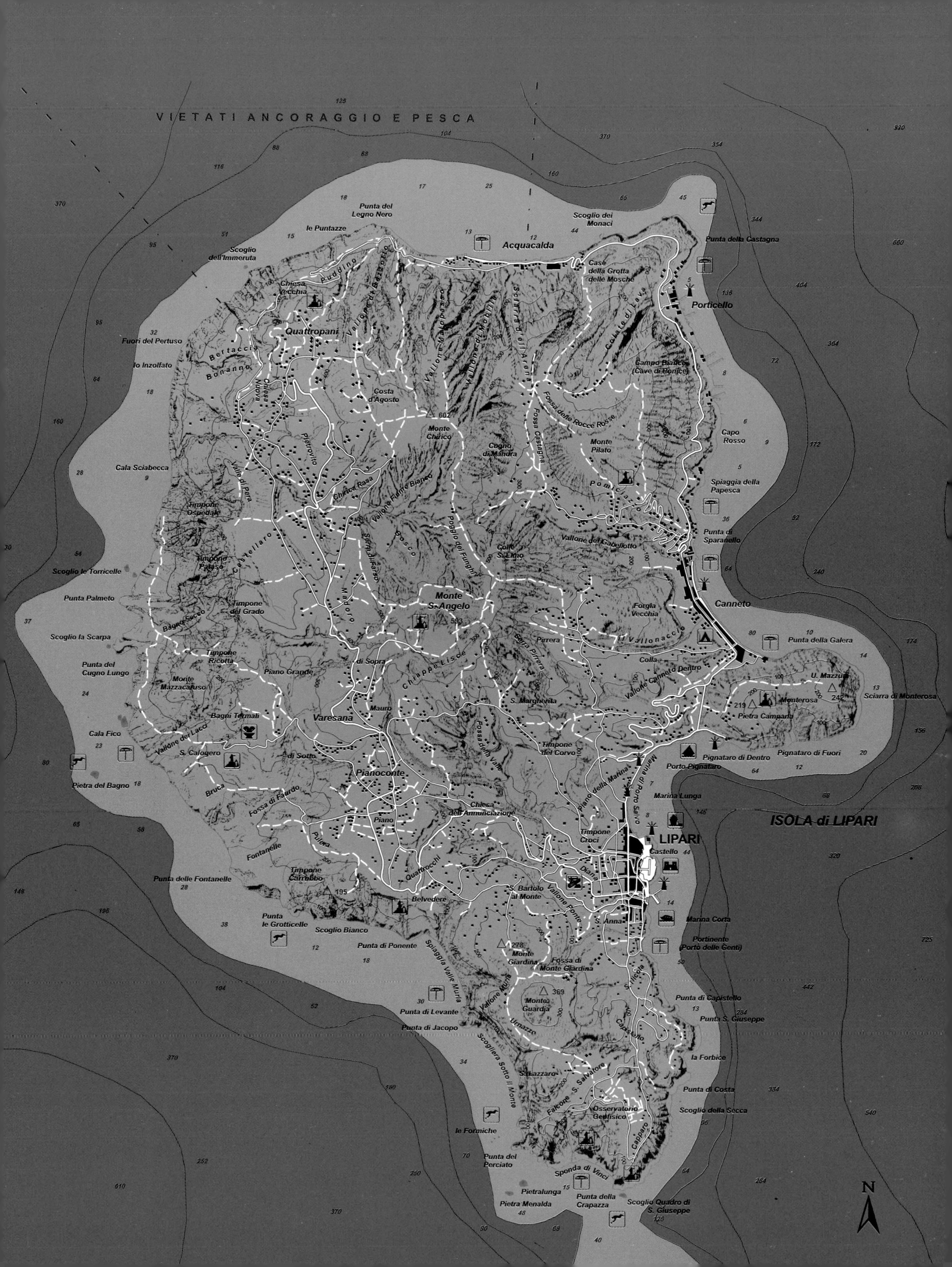

VIETATI ANCORAGGIO E PESCA
ISOLA di LIPARI
LIPARI
Punta del Legno Nero
le Puntazze
Acquacalda
Scoglio dei Monaci
Punta della Castagna
Scoglio dell'Immeruta
Chiesa Vecchia
Quattropani
Fuori del Pertuso
Bertaccia
Bonanno
Costa d'Agosto
Monte Chirico
Case della Grotta delle Mosche
Porticello
Campo Bianco (Cave di Pomice)
Fossa delle Rocce Rosse
Monte Pilato
Capo Rosso
Cala Sciabecca
Cogno di Mandra
Spiaggia della Papesca
Timpone Ospedale
Chirica Rasa
Vallone Fiume Bianco
Pomiciazzo
Punta di Sparanello
Vallone del Gabellotto
Colle S. Elmo
Poggio dei Funghi
Timpone Pataso
Castellaro
Scoglio le Torricelle
Punta Palmeto
Monte S. Angelo
Forgia Vecchia
Canneto
Timpone del Grado
Bagno Secco
Scoglio la Scarpa
Vallonaccio
Punta della Galera
Pirrera
Serra Pirrera
Colla
Timpone Ricotta
Piano Grande
Punta del Cugno Lungo
Monte Mazzacaruso
Chiappe Lisce
Vallone Canneto Dentro
U. Mazzuca
Sciarra di Monterosa
Monterosa
Pietra Campana
S. Margherita
Varesana
Mauro
Bagni Termali
Cala Fico
Vallone dei Lacci
S. Calogero
di Sotto
Timpone del Corvo
Pignataro di Dentro
Pignataro di Fuori
Porto Pignataro
Pietra del Bagno
Pianoconte
Marina di Porto Salvo
Piano della Marina
Marina Lunga
Bruca
Fossa di Faardo
Chiesa dell'Annunciazione
Timpone Croci
Castello
Fontanelle
Piano
Punta delle Fontanelle
Timpone Carrubbo
Quattrocchi
S. Bartolo al Monte
Vallone Ponte
Belvedere
S. Anna
Marina Corta
Punta le Grotticelle
Scoglio Bianco
Punta di Ponente
Spiaggia Valle Muria
Monte Giardina
Fossa di Monte Giardina
Portinente (Porto delle Genti)
Monte Guardia
Punta di Capistello
Punta di Levante
Punta S. Giuseppe
Punta di Jacopo
Urnazzo
Capistello
Scogliera Sotto il Monte
la Forbice
S. Lazzaro
S. Salvatore
Falcone
Punta di Costa
Osservatorio Geofisico
Scoglio della Secca
le Formiche
Punta del Perciato
Sponda di Vinci
Pietralunga
Pietra Menalda
Punta della Crapazza
Scoglio Quadro di S. Giuseppe
N

Salina is a surprising island with much to offer. The sense of serenity and beauty of the place also deeply affected **Massimo Troisi,** who made his last film, *Il Postino*, here. It isn't a worldly place, which "lights up" two weeks a year for rushed tourists, but a living island which still cultivates its fields and increases its production of **malmsey**. All over the world this "nectar of the Gods" is know as "Malmsey of Lipari", but the principal place of production is Malfa di Salina. **Capers** are a symbol of the Eolian islands, but only on Salina are there extensive crops. A living island which has set up a nature reserve to protect two extinct volcanoes covered with thick vegetation: Fossa delle Felci and Monte Pirri.

The Greeks called it **Didyme** (twins) because of the presence of these volcanoes, separated by the plateau of Valdichiesa. The present name derives from the *saline*, now a brackish lake, which extends along the coast towards Lipari. The salt produced here was indispensable and was used to preserve fish and capers.

There are three principal villages, the districts of **Santa Marina, Malfa** and **Leni.**

Three art galleries and a museum on such a small island is surprising only to those who know nothing of the history of Salina. The inhabitants have always been enterprising and industrious and indeed at the end of the 1800's its merchant fleet numbered 150 sailing ships.

Above: house at Pollara used in the filming of "Il Postino"

Below: view of Salina from Lipari

Opposite page: vines and the sea at Capo Faro

29

101

The principal port for ferries and hydrofoils is that of **Santa Marina**, where a small port for pleasure craft is also being built. On the other side of the island you land at Rinella. A good bus service connects the villages until late in the evening. The roads are narrow but tarmacked. Santa Marina is spread out at the foot of **Monte Fossa delle Felci** and **Monte Rivi.** You immediately notice the characteristic bell-towers of the 18th century Chiesa di Santa Marina. The mountains were once a refuge for the inhabitants when Saracen pirate ships arrived. Above Santa Marina a path climbs up from **Serro dell'Acqua** to the **caves** dug out of the tuff. Some of them are connected. It is a pleasant walk among olive and fruit orchards and, after a steep climb, you discover some of these refuges are inhabited. Two kilometres to the south is **Lingua**, a small fishing village which offers simple and authentic hospitality, with good restaurants serving excellent local fish dishes. Don't miss Alfredo's excellent *granite.*

Before reaching Lingua you can observe an **18th century bridge** in the Zappini gorge, near the sea. It is part of an old stone road, no longer used which local people have recently uncovered. The lake at Lingua is very picturesque, with its **lighthouse**.

This is the greenest island of the archipelago and we recommend, to those who love walking, a day on Monte Fossa delle Felci to admire, from the top of Salina, the other islands and even Etna.

It is possible to climb up from Santa Marina, Lingua or **Valdichiesa**. From Lingua it takes 2-3 hours, but is quite a difficult climb. A lot of steps take you to the peak of Menavento and, after having passed vines and uncultivated land on steep paths, you reach the summit at 968 metres. The mountain is more accessible from Valdichiesa. In this case you have to visit the **Santuario della Madonna del Terzito**: it is a place of worship and prayer where first there was a chapel in the 5th century, a church in the 7th century and then a sanctuary in the 17th century. There are some important votive offerings. They are paintings on glass representing a valuable example of popular art. A short stretch of road, with a few bends, takes you from Santa Marina to Malfa, on the northern coast, after passing vines and rugged gorges. Malfa is the biggest village on the island and is situated near the **Valle di Giovi** which goes down to the sea between **Monte Porri** and **Monte Rivi.**

(To be continued page 82)

In alto: ponte del'700 nel Vallone Zappini

A fianco: Santuario della Madonna del Terzito

Pagina a destra: in alto, il pittoresco lago di Lingua con il faro

In basso, abitato e lago di Lingua

SALINA, TRAVELLING THROUGH TIME

A walk through the places where the remains of ancient civilisations have been found, apart from the natural beauty of the countryside, lets us hear echoes from the past opening up exciting scenarios.

On Salina a prehistoric settlement has been found bearing witness to the human presence on the island since the last centuries of the 5th millenium BC. The oldest settlement, dating back to that time and similar to the one at Castellaro on Lipari, has recently been found at Rinella, in the district of Leni. There is a hut and a great deal of obsidian splinters, imported from Lipari, showing that tools were produced for export to the Western Mediterranean.

On the summit of Monte Fossa delle Felci and at Brigadiere, apart from obsidian splinters, fragments of Diana style pottery (circa 3000 BC) have been found along with other archaeological artefacts which demonstrate human presence on Salina since neolithic times.

Eneolithic pottery fragments in Pianoconte style (circa 2500 BC) have also come from this dig, as well as the remains of huts of the Piano Quartura culture dating back to the last centuries of the 3rd millenium BC.

Previously, at Malfa, funeral attire of this culture had been found, at Santa Maria in the locality of Policastro, a cup, probably part of tomb attire and, at Serro dell'Acqua, remains of huts.

In the Bronze Age, from the last century of the 3rd millennium BC onwards, Salina was populated by people from mainland Greece, probably the Eoli of ancient legends, and then by people from Sicily, where the civilisation of Thaspos was flourishing. The settlements made by the former group, belonging to the culture of Capo Graziano, and used for more than half a millenium (almost until the end of the 15th century BC), have been discovered in various parts of the island, chosen particularly for security reasons. In particular at Megna (early Bronze Age), Serro Brigadiere (Early and Middle Bronze Age) and at Serro dei Cianfi (Middle Bronze Age). The settlement used by populations from Sicily, belongs to the Milazzese civilisation (from the second half of the 15th century BC to the first half of the 13th century BC) and was found at Portella. It is believed to have been destroyed by the Ausoni (around 1270 BC), a population from the coast of Campania who are referred to in the legends handed down to us from Diodoro Siculo. After this violent destruction, the island of Salina seems to have been uninhabited until the 50th Olympiad (580/576 BC), when a group of Greeks, of Dorian origin, coming from Cnido, settled on Lipari.

The Liparesi, settlers from Cnidi, began to cultivate the fertile land of Salina, called Dydime by the Greeks, according to Thucydides, so the island was permanently settled from the beginning of the 4th century BC like the other islands. The most important settlement developed at Santa Marina and part of the walls of an imperial age house are visible on the beach, at the end of the sea-front. From that time on, for more than a thousand years, there were Greek, Roman and Byzantine settlements, up to the Arab conquest of the islands in 838 AD. From then, until the 16th century, the only evidence of human presence on the island is the late Medieval settlement at Serro Perciato in the district of Santa Marina.

In 729 Sir Willibald (brother of Santa Valpurga), returning from a pilgrimage to the Holy Land, stopped at Lipari to venerate the remains of St. Bartholomew. Finding the crater of Monte Pelato in eruption, he had to spend the night on Salina, at that time more heavily populated than Lipari. In Byzantine times the island took its present name because of the presence of a lake of brackish water on the East coast, where a saline was set up in the third century BC. The oldest remains have recently been found above the lake, with fragments of pottery and walls of Roman buildings ("opus reticulatum" walls in the lake are represented in a print by Houel).

Graeco-Roman and Byzantine remains have been found in various parts of the island: around Santa Marina, pottery fragments of the 5th century BC at Serro dell'Acqua, classic age tombs at Barone, a classic age column re-used in Byzantine times above the sea-front and now kept in the Town Hall, late Roman tombs above the port and at Mastrognoli in the district of Lingua; around Malfa, Hellenistic tombs near the power station (one has been rebuilt in the school yard), a late Hellenistic funeral inscription (now in the Civic Musem of Santa Marina) at Capo Faro, and late Hellenistic and Roman tombs at Capo Gramignazzi; around Leni, terracottas of the 4th and 3rd centuries BC, Roman pottery and tombs at Valdichiesa (some have been rebuilt next to the art gallery of Valdichiesa and are probably connected to a settlement, situated on the site of the present football pitch). The artefacts discovered are today largely housed in the smaller islands section of the Archaeological Museum of Lipari. On Salina, you can only visit the few ruins we have mentioned, awaiting the activation of a number of archaeological itineraries. The settlements found have been covered to protect them from further deterioration. Despite the remarkable transformations, the inhabitants of the island haven't lost their identity and the island has not become an anonymous holiday village, with no cultural background. This is certainly connected to its ancient history that can, in part, be re-lived, visiting the small Civic Museum of Santa Marina, where some objects are displayed.

Riccardo Gullo

NAVALPESCA
SPORT
REGIONE SICILIANA

SALINA AND MALMSEY

"Near the island of Lipari, a mile to the west is another island called Salina where there are beautiful vines not of wine grapes but zibibbo grapes, where large quantities are made and exported as far as Constantinople."

This was written by the abbot Gerolamo Maurando who arrived in the islands following the pirate Ariadeno Barbarossa in the summer of 1544 and gives us important evidence of the flourishing economic activity of Salina. The presence of vines, however, shouldn't deceive us into believing there were organised communities on the island. The continuing presence of pirates had depopulated the island since the Byzantine age and the persistent lack of fortifications had forced the Liparesi to visit only for looking after and harvesting the vines, as Campis wrote in the 1600's.

The repopulation of Salina, after centuries of abandonment began at the end of the 1500's encouraged by the concessions of the Bishop of Lipari, eager to put the fertile land of the eastern side and the plateau under cultivation, it intensified at the end of the 18th century and reached a peak in the mid 1800's. In the space of 300 years men and families from all over the lower Tyrrhenian came together in the communities based around the churches of S. Marina in the east, of MM. SS. del Terzito in the south, San Lorenzo in the north and Sant'Onofrio in the west. Attracted by the mirage of land or the possibility of long term work, they had different stories and motivations. Without an established patrimonial position, it was to be expected that a community without common origins and traditions would be dependent on the main island, very close at hand and with a strong consolidated economic structure. Indeed, the life of Salina was linked to that of Lipari in many aspects. In the early 19th century conditions finally permitted the new community to take control of the local economy out of the hands of Lipari traders,and those of the area of the Stretto, who imposed their own prices in colonial style. It was the sudden increase in demand for malmsey in the early 1800's that gave Salina its new strength in trade. The malmsey was required by the 10,000 English soldiers in Messina, trying to face a possible advance of Napoleon in Sicily. For 10 years, the commissaries of the British army requested the malmsey and put it on the officers' tables. This initiated a process of economic development, as a good part of the revenue was re-invested in the cultivation of new lands and strengthe-

ning of links with the whole Mediterranean.
These investments allowed the inhabitants to exploit the productive potential of the land to the maximum, and the shipowners to plan ways of consolidating wider profit margins. From port to port they traded in everything to invest in new vines. The growing wealth also allowed the villages to free themselves from the administrative power of Lipari in the mid 1800's. In the second half of the century small shipping companies were set up running large sailing ships which marked the new expansion. So in the 1870's the population neared 9,000 inhabitants.
The end of the cycle was coming dramatically close. Between 1870 and 1885 the phylloxera parasite invaded the whole of Europe, destroying the vines and, in spring 1889, put an end to the illusions of the islanders and those who thought that 23 miles of sea would stop an aphid. Emigration started up and in 15 years the population halved.
The 1900's brought new strategies and alternatives. Emigrants' revenues helped set up banks, production and work co-operatives, the electric company and the steamers of the "Eolia", but it was not enough. The rules of the game had changed and the few miles of sea that divide the island from the mainland had become an ocean. In the archipelago only the pumice quarrying industry enjoyed a natural monopoly and gave life-blood to the biggest island, the rest survived with aid or died. It was this way for the Eolia shipping company, run by the sons of the original owners. It was born and prospered, protected by the pro-Fascist archbishop of Messina, Mons. Angelo Paino, also from Salina and originating from a family of navigators.
With the fall of the regime, however, the association collapsed along with the economic and political framework on which it was based.
It was necessary to wait for the 1970's until a new type of development began, based on tourism. In this new era the islanders, decimated by decades of emigration, don't have sufficient cultural instruments to face the problems created by this new resource.
However, with the first environmental problems it was realised that the tourist industry had to follow the practice of the illuminated merchants of the past, not to destroy the patrimony of the island and create widespread wealth and work through family businesses. This is the road followed today.
There is, however, the danger of considering tourism as a monoculture, forgetting that a hundred years ago, ruin was caused by concentrating on just one resource (vines). For this reason it seems to be more important than ever to develop and commercially plan the agriculture sector side by side with tourism.

Marcello Saija.

CLIMBING FOSSA DELLE FELCI

Climbing to the summit of Fossa delle Felci, you can admire the island of Salina as a whole. The various types of coast originate from the two, very different volcanoes. Monte Porri is rugged and wild, while Monte Fossa is green and luxuriant. The latter can only be climbed on foot.
Passing the end of the road above Valdichiesa, the air, full of smells of the trees and plants, helps you to forget the hard climb. The countryside and climate change, becoming first like on a hill and on top like a mountain.
To face the three-hour walk, it is better to start off early, before it gets too hot, or, if you intend to stay the night on the mountain, in the late afternoon. Rich heather, mastic trees and euphorbias welcome you along the path which takes you through the wood, full of chestnut trees, oaks, pines and strawberry trees, which reach a height of seven to eight metres. In spring the whole ridge is livened by the warm yellow of the broom a spectacular colour effect, an explosion of nature in the most fertile ground of the archipelago. The strong scent of flowers accompanies us on our way and, between the trees, you can't help glimpsing the sea, always different, and Panarea, Stromboli, Filicudi, Alicudi, Vulcano and Lipari as if it were possible to stretch out a hand and touch them. On the way, before each bend, there are narrow paths which let you shorten the distance. Across the most rugged part of the mountain, towards the Santuario della Madonna del Terzito, there are paths which, once, were the only ways of reaching the top, but are advisable only for tough walkers. Along the paths there are steps, cut out of the ground. The steps are made from large stones and old tree trunks, which cover this side of the mountain and are the only possible things to hold on to.
All around nature invites you to take a closer look at the plant life. Some rare trees found here are the holm oak, which once formed an impenetrable forest all over the island. The feeling of peace and tranquillity during the climb is to be relished. In the sight of pines, oaks and so on you should feel part of a complex world, worthy of greater respect. Almost at the top, a sudden stop in the walk, attracts your eyes to

the horizon. This happens because of the fire barrier which rounds the whole of Monte Fossa, taking away part of its green mantle.
The countryside changes continuously. The thick vegetation gives way to steppe and rocks. You can also look up to catch a glimpse of another surprise offered by Monte Fossa. It is Eleonora's falcon, the symbol of Salina for naturalists, with spectacular flying techniques and an imposing wing span. It is a very rare bird and looks like a fast black mark in the bright blue sky. After the steppe, you find the ferns, a small short group, which increase in number and size as you approach the crater.
Reaching a viewpoint on the edge of the crater, large rocks of white and red colouring appear out of the brush. From here you just get a glimpse of the seven pearls of the Mediterranean. Stromboli, with its plume, is the most spectacular. The perfect cone shape, the crater surrounded by an often menacing cloud, give it a fairy-tale air. Monte Porri is equally spectacular in its impressiveness. you are on the highest volcano of the entire archipelago (968 metres), its crater is 100 metres deep and has a diameter of 600-700 metres.

Here there are more ferns. They border the paths, invade the crater, more and more, bigger and bigger. They surround you, taking you into a world of gnomes, elves, fairies and whatever your imagination creates. It seems as if nature asks us to forget ailments, pain, disappointments, boredom, desperation and sadness and to rejoice in its appearance on Monte Fossa.
It doesn't matter if, instead of a gnome, you meet a dormouse, or, instead of an elf, a wild rabbit. These are, in any case, inhabitants of the wood that are very difficult to see.
Nights on the Fossa are full of magic and romanticism; a warm sleeping bag and a glass of malmsey are all you need, the rest is done by the charm of being in a crater at night, surrounded by giant chestnut trees. Between the branches, the stars are like little lights fighting off the dark, while the singing of the crickets counts the seconds, allowing us to forget time and concentrate on infinity.
On awakening, early in the morning, the spell vanishes. Daylight pushes between the leafy branches of the chestnuts and it is almost a duty to go to the edge of the crater to watch the sunrise. One by one, as if by magic, the other islands appear on the horizon, reminding us that another day has begun and it is time to go down and face new adventures in the Eolian islands.

Amelia Ruggeri

Opposite page: valley of Valdichiesa and Monte Porri

Above: Monte Fossa delle Felci

(Continued from page 74)

Its name probably comes from the **Amalfitani** who emigrated here in the 12th century, attracted by the incentives offered by the Normans to repopulate the islands. **Malvasia** vines are cultivated, as well as capers, and raisins (la **passulina**) are produced. Fishing has always been important and now tourism, which increases every year. The little port, called **Scalo Galera**, is only suitable for small craft. There is a concrete slipway to pull up fishing boats. On the night of San Lorenzo it is lit up by a firework display, in honour of the patron. Moving on from Malfa the road climbs up the slopes of Monte Porri and, after a final bend, you are on the plateau of **Pollara**, with its small scattered houses: it is a natural amphitheatre, of volcanic origin, with a sheer drop to the sea. It is all that remains of the largest crater of the islands, with a diameter of more than 1 km. A fertile sunny hollow, bordered by Monte Porri. The principal resource for the 60 inhabitants is the caper picking from May to August.

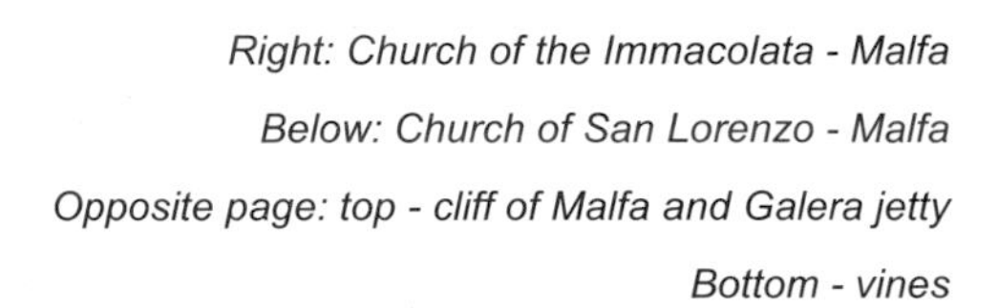

Right: Church of the Immacolata - Malfa

Below: Church of San Lorenzo - Malfa

Opposite page: top - cliff of Malfa and Galera jetty

Bottom - vines

The bay is closed to the north by a promontory, **"Perciato"**, worn down by the sea which breaks against it incessantly. You can see the boat shelters dug out of the tuff by fishermen. Out to sea is a crag, left behind by geological subsidence, and, in the distance, Filicudi and Alicudi.
To reach the beach, possibly the loveliest in the islands, you pass behind the church and follow a tarmac road for about a kilometre. Malfa district council plans to name the new beach road after Massimo Troisi.
In 1994 the film **Il Postino** (the Postman), based on a

novel by Antonio Skarmeta and inspired by the exile of Pablo Neruda, was set at Pollara. It was filmed in the house of an artist, Pippo Cafarella, used as the dwelling of the Chilean poet played by Philippe Noiret. The house is an attraction for many visitors every year, charmed by the film, the rustling of the wind and the peace of this place. The countryside is full of broom, heather and caper flowers.
The last part of our itinerary takes us to **Rinella** and **Leni**. Leni, called Lenoi by the Greeks, comes from the name of the containers for crushing grapes, obviously grown even then. It is spread out on the plateau between the two volcanoes and enjoys a cooler climate, while allowing summer visitors to reach the beach at Rinella in a few minutes. Today the village of Rinella has grown, but a few decades ago it was a few fishermen's cottages, the landing place and boat shelters dug out of the tuff, near the beach.

DISCOVERING THE SEA

Sailing round the island by boat is the best way to admi-

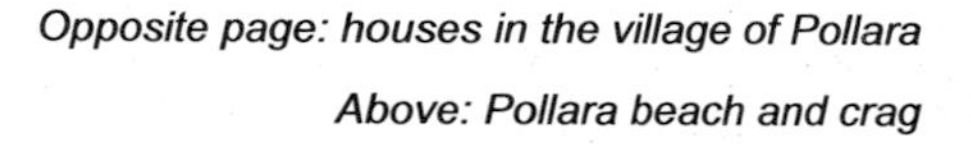

Opposite page: houses in the village of Pollara

Above: Pollara beach and crag

re the beaches and rocky coastline. For boat rental contact at Malfa: **Rametta** (tel. 9844010) and **Ministeri** (tel. 9844233); at Santa Marina: **Nautica Levante** (tel. 9843083), **Follone** and **Zavone** (tel. 9843189), **Arlotta** (tel. 9843094) and **Saltamacchia** (tel. 9843160). For **diving** contact **Centro Nautico Salina** (tel. 9809033) at Rinella.

Heading towards **Capo Faro**, in an anti-clockwise direction, the coast is, at first, rugged and sheer. There is a small landing place at the Capo and, if you have enough breath, a stairway up to the lighthouse. Passing by the impressive gorges of the mountains, you reach the **jetty of Galera** and in the distance **Punta del Perciato**. We are in the surprisingly lovely **bay of Pollara**, where you can make a stop on the beach. It is better not to get too close to the cliffs because of the risk of falling rocks. For divers **la Secca di Pollara** is ideal, underwater mountains rich in fish life. The alternate coloured rock stratifications bear witness to successive eruptions. The edge of the water, today partially submerged, was probably near the large crag (**il Faraglione**) which stands in the centre of the bay.

Opposite page: top - Church of St. Gaetano and building at Leni

Bottom - village and port of Rinella

Above: boats on Rinella beach and shelters dug in the tuff

The bay is closed by **Filo di Branda,** impressive red coloured sheer rocks. The coast is overlooked by Monte Porri. After Praiola is the cave of **Racina** and then **Punta Marcello** and **Punta Megna**. Along the coast you reach **Rinella** and a large beach with the **Tre Pini campsite**, a liberty style building (the Hotel **Ariana**), the jetty and the **caves** cut out of the rocks. Further on the coast is straight under Fossa delle Felci. At **Punta Tre Pietre** you can moor the boat for an interesting underwater excursion. Rounding **Punta Grottuzza**, you reach Lingua with the lighthouse and lake. The coast is now flat as you approach Santa Marina again.

SHOPPING

Capers, olives, oil, jams, honey and malmsey will help you to remember Salina, its clear sea, flowers and beautiful sunsets.

These typical products can be bought in one of the many shops on the island or direct from the producers.

At Lingua the farm belonging to Carlo **Hauner** (tel. 9843141), a vine-grower for 30 years and responsible for the re-birth of malmsey; the **Sapori del Mediterraneo** (tel. 9843141). At Malfa the farms **Carrà** (tel. 9844051), **Caravaglio** (tel. 9844368), **Venti del Sud**

(tel. 9844079), **Sant'Anna** (tel. 9844167) and **l'agriturismo Sant'Onofrio** (tel. 9844143). At **Santa Marina** you find: the pottery and souvenir shop of Felicia **Lauria** where you can find all you need for boating and fishing, and that of Signora **Salmeri**; the supermarket **Carpe Diem**, clothing and particular basketwork gifts from **Malizia**, jewellery and antique furniture from **Indigo** and typical sweets from **Cambusa**.

At **Lingua**, the *granite* from **Alfredo**. At **Malfa**, you can buy antique furniture and gifts from **A Putia**, typical Eolian sweets from **Cose Duci**, *granite*, typical sweets, newpapers and magazines at the **bar Malvasia,** which is also a public telephone point.

At **Leni, Cappadona** for food, **Chiofalo** for ice-cream and **Mirenda** for everything you need.

WHERE TO STAY

To book typical Eolian houses or apartments you can contact the travel agency **Dydime** at Santa Marina (tel. 9843410) and **New Immobiliare** at Malfa (tel. 9844168).

Opposite page: top - Ceriantus - Punta Tre Pietre

Bottom - cliffs below Secca del Capo

Right: Galera jetty - Malfa

Below: Lingua lighthouse and its sparkling sea

AT MALFA

• HOTEL SIGNUM♥♥♥: In a garden near the sea, a romantic Eolian style hotel (tel. 9844222).

• PUNTA SCARIO♥♥: A white Eolian building above the sea with a view of Panarea and Stromboli (tel. 9844139).

• VILLAGGIO CAPO FARO♥: Eolian style houses (tel. 9844330).

• RESIDENCE SANTA ISABEL: Apartments with one or more rooms in a new Eolian style complex.

AT SANTA MARIA

• MAMMA SANTINA♥: Panoramic family guest house (tel. 9843054).

• PUNTA BARONE♥: Welcoming hotel, near the sea (tel. 9843054).

Also recommended: rented rooms from Buccafusa (tel. 9843022).

AT LINGUA

• LA MARINARA♥: On the sea-front (tel. 9843022).

• A CANNATA: Lovely villas in Eolian style (tel. 9843161).

• RESIDENCE DELLE FRESIE: Near the lake (tel. 9843049).

AT RINELLA

• L'ARIANA♥♥: Old liberty style villa on the cliffs. Pleasant environment and good service (tel. 9809075).

Recommended: rooms for rent from **Sea Side** (tel. 9809023).

WHAT TO EAT

AT SANTA MARINA

• PORTOBELLO: Romantic terrace overlooking the sea

with typical home cooking. Spaghetti "al fuoco", raw grouper "alla Portobello" and sweet and sour fish.

- DA FRANCO: On a hill with a beautiful view and a wide choice of hors d'oeuvres. Maccheroni "alla Franco" and fish cooked in paper or salt.
- LA CAMBUSA: Opposite the ferry quay. Specialities: linguine "al cartoccio con polpa di ricci", mussels, clams and fish soup.
- MAMMA SANTINA: Fish with sweet and sour onions, spaghetti with 13 herbs and tomato, white bream with filling.
- PUNTA BARONE: Typical Eolian cuisine, fresh fish.

Also recommended:the pizzerias Matarazzo, Napoletana and Rago.

AT LINGUA

- A CANNATA: On a terrace, offers penne "alla salinara" with peppers, pine-seeds, capers and olives; homemade maccheroni with aubergines, swordfish roulades and stuffed squid with malmsey.
- IL GAMBERO: On a terrace with a tank full of lobsters, serves spaghetti "alla eoliana", with anchovies, basil, capers, olives and tuna; barbecued lobster.
- IL DELFINO: Two terraces near the sea. Recommended: sea-food hors d'oeuvres, spaghetti with lobster, mixed grill or fish soup.

AT MALFA

- HOTEL SIGNUM: Eolian and international cuisine of high level.
- VILLAGGIO CAPO FARO: Pizzerias A Lumaredda and La Ginestra.

AT RINELLA

- L'ARIANA: Offers "lasagnette all'eoliana" with capers, fish cooked in salt and grouper "al cartoccio".
- DA PEPPINO

We also recommend the pizzerias **Da Marco** and **Salina Village**.

After dinner at Santa Marina people meet up on the corso at the pub **'Nni Lausta** with live music or at the disco **La Cambusa**. At Rinella at the bar of the Hotel **L'Ariana** and at **Salina Village**, open till late.

Left above - Sunset in Pollara

Bottom - characteristic shaped hills on Salina

Below: port and village of S. Marina Salina

RELIGIOUS FESTIVALS AND LADEN TABLES

The cult of the Madonna del Terzito, which has lasted more than a thousand years, is widespread above all on Salina, the other islands and among the Eolian islanders spread all over the world. The origins date back to the first centuries of Christianity. The story that an oriental monk, to escape persecution took refuge in the thick woods of Valdichiesa, has been handed down. In this place, after the hermit's death, an image of the Madonna was found and a church was built.
The term 'Terzito' derives from the Spanish 'Tersillo', three rings of the bell which accompanied and accompanies prayers and which, according to local legend, some foresters heard in 1622, in the valley where a new church dedicated to the Madonna appeared, on the remains of the first, after centuries of neglect.
On this island, this devotion is also testified by the presence of small chapels and shrines along streets and paths and by offerings, oil paintings and paintings on glass dating back to the 18th century and the beginning of the 19th century, preserved today in the sanctuary at Valdichiesa.
On July 23rd every year, celebrations in honour of the Madonna del Terzito take place with great participation and religious fervour. The statue of the Madonna is carried in procession through the streets of the village and the church square is full of lights, voices, stalls and people.

August 10th is dedicated to St. Lorenzo, the patron of Malfa. Once, the main streets of the village were decorated with flower arches, flags and multicoloured lights that were in harmony with the colours of the countryside, the gardens and the houses spread over the Malfa plateau.
Even today, a band passes through the village streets and at noon, which is preceded by a joyful pealing of the bells, devotees of the saint ritually dig the earth with their hands in search of pieces of coal. In fact, St. Lorenzo was burnt alive and therefore, any finds are considered as a miraculous sign. The procession as far as the parish church square, and the customary fireworks, which illuminate the night, conclude the festival.
Every year, in honour of St. Joseph at Malfa on March 19th and at Leni on May 1st, the church square is traditionally prepared for "a tavuliata": a long table spread with food.
At Malfa the tradition dates back to 1835, the year in which some sailors prayed to St. Giuseppe to save them during a storm at sea.
Arriving safe and sound, they decided to offer pasta and chick peas, cooked in big copper pans, "i quadari", to poor people.
The custom has endured over the years and today, all families in the village prepare food: typical Aeolian dishes, pasta and chick peas, seafood, lobsters, meat, wine, desserts and fruit.
A small orchestra accentuates the joyful atmosphere while, St. Joseph, the Madonna and baby Jesus, in period costume, participate in the festival. It is a unique festival because all the village is united around the banquet, in the churchyard: the whole community.

Antonio Brundu

Opposite page: Santuario della Madonna del Terzito at Valdichiesa

Left: "Tavuliata" of S. Giuseppe - Malfa

Above: "Tavuliata" of S. Giuseppe - Leni

THE CAPER

The caper, whose name comes from the Arabic “cabr” or “cabir” is from the Asiatic, subtropical area.
Every year, in the first week of June, a feast in its honour is held in Salina, organized by the Dydime Cultural Association.
Maybe not everyone knows that capers are the flowers of the plant still in bud.
If left to blossom, they are very beautiful flowers, elegant and fragile, exotic.
The fruit is called “cocunci” and looks like a gherkin. If you can see the plant in flower it means that the cultivation has been neglected.
Every flower is a caper not picked.
In the Eolian Islands there are two varieties: the “nocella” and the “nocellara”, whose fruit, since time immemorial has been put in salt to give it a particular taste. The ground, the cultivation, the air , the method of preservation, make the caper of Salina a unique and unrepeatable product, the very emblem of the island. It is the main character of Eolian cuisine, you will find it in starters, salads, pasta, flavourings for second courses, or simply on its own with homemade bread, just out of the oven.
But the caper isn’t only a pleasure to eat. Even in the 1600’s a treatise extolled its curative properties. It kindled appetite, lowered blood pressure and mitigated toothache.
There is another quality of the caper not to be underestimated: it seems to rekindle another kind of appetite!
This belief is widespread in the Mediterranean area and is part of popular tradition.
In any case, its therapeutic properties for lowering cholesterol have recently been discovered.

SALINA: APHRODISIAC CUISINE

A land so rich in smells, scents, colours and contrasts had to have a strong cuisine. Strong not in the sense of robust, but sensual. Almost all the recipes of the island have this characteristic. The important and constant presence of the caper gives every dish the same sensuality of the plant, the slight fleshiness of the flower, the famous potentiality of the fruit. Dishes rich in colour and warmth, which you devour with your eyes before tasting them. The colours are an integral and irreplaceable part of the dishes. The shades of dark green, typical of the caper, fade away with the light red of the tomatoes, with the intense green of the basil and of the mint, the dazzling white of garlic, with the violet stripes of the onion, with the yellow of the lemon peel, the yellow/green oil.
Every dish is an invitation to pleasure.
To enjoy fully these sensations, in all their complexity, you should go to Salina in spring.

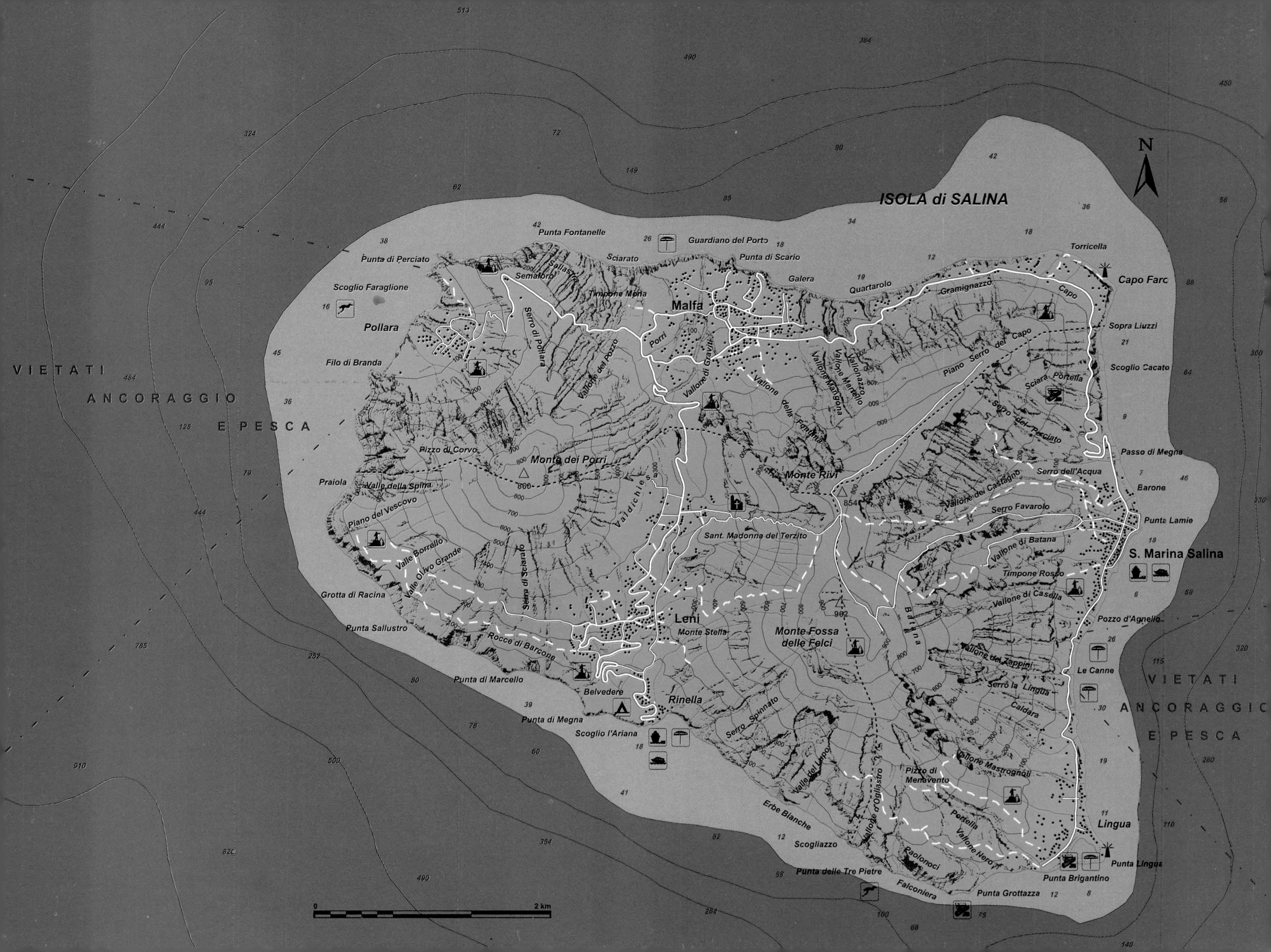

ISOLA di SALINA
N
VIETATI ANCORAGGIO E PESCA
VIETATI ANCORAGGIO E PESCA
Capo Faro
Torricella
Capo
Gramignazzo
Quartarolo
Galera
Punta di Scario
Guardiano del Porto
Sciarato
Punta Fontanelle
Timpone Mona
Semaforo
Sallastra
Punta di Perciato
Scoglio Faraglione
Pollara
Filo di Branda
Serro di Pollara
Vallone del Pozzo
Malfa
Porri
Vallone di Gravili
Vallone della Fontana
Vallone Mangona
Vallone Martello
Vallonazzo
Piano Serro del Capo
Sopra Liuzzi
Scoglio Cacato
Sciara Portella
Serro del Perciato
Passo di Megna
Serro dell'Acqua
Barone
Vallone dei Castagno
Serro Favarolo
Punta Lamie
S. Marina Salina
Vallone di Batana
Timpone Rosso
Vallone di Casella
Pozzo d'Agnello
Batana
Vallone dei Zappini
Le Canne
Serro la Lingua
Caldara
Vallone Mastrognoli
Pizzo di Menavento
Portella
Vallone Nero
Lingua
Punta Lingua
Punta Brigantino
Punta Grottazza
Paolonoci
Falconiera
Punta delle Tre Pietre
Vallone d'Ogliastro
Scogliazzo
Erbe Bianche
Valle del Lupo
Serro Spinnato
Monte Fossa delle Felci
Monte Rivi
Sant. Madonna del Terzito
Leni
Monte Stella
Rinella
Scoglio l'Ariana
Punta di Megna
Belvedere
Punta di Marcello
Rocce di Barcone
Serra di Sciarato
Valdichiesa
Monte dei Porri
Pizzo di Corvo
Praiola
Valle della Spina
Piano del Vescovo
Valle Borrello
Valle Olivo Grande
Grotta di Racina
Punta Sallustro
0
2 km

A HIDDEN WORLD

In the last two million years more than 10000 volcanoes have been formed on the earth and more than 500 have had eruptions which have been spoken about through history.
The following millennium of magic rituals, sacrifices, prayers and offerings testify to the terror and also the deep respect that man has always had for these forces of nature. The volcano, in fact, has not only been an instrument of death and destruction, but also a source of energy and life.
Until recently volcanic eruptions were therefore considered as an unlucky destiny or connected to the wrath of local divinities. But man easily forgets, so only a few decades of inactivity are enough for a volcano to be considered extinct. In reality the average life of a volcano is thousands of years, even pauses of hundreds of years are really ephemeral.
Research into the field of vulcanology has developed over the last 70-80 years, even if the first attempts at a scientific approach date back to the end of the last century.
The efforts of the scientific community are concentrated on the possibility of reducing 'risk', deriving from eruption, working on the evaluation of a "probability" parameter connected to the knowledge of volcanic activity from all possible points of view.
The island of Vulcano today represents the only example in the world of an active volcano under constant monitoring.
The necessity for such control is clear if we recall some of the most violent eruptions of our time: Mt. Pinatubo (the Philippines), Paracutin (Colombia), Unzen (Japan) and Mt. St. Helens (USA). These volcanoes have shown an explosive activity which, as has been ascertained, has had serious consequences compared to the effusion of Hawaiian volcanoes or, for example, Etna. Volcanoes in Italy have a pre-eminently explosive activity and are found mostly in proximity to inhabited centres, factors which heighten the risk.
Volcanic surveillance has been continuing for no longer than 20 years but the commitment of researchers has allowed a great amount of information, regarding not only surface volcanic activity, but also underwater activity to be obtained.
The archipelago of the Aeolian islands represents a rich and surprising area for volcanic activity under the surface of the sea.
Investigations have developed mainly in the waters of those islands in which the emanation of different types of gas has been noticed. Particularly intense fumaroles on Vulcano with a ground temperature of 500°C, weak gas emanations on Lipari and Panarea and no sign of gas emanation on the other islands.
The Aeolian islands emerge from the sea to varying heights of a few hundred metres (Panarea) to about one thousand metres (Stromboli and Salina).
Considering the fact that these islands reach depths of 1500/2000 metres, scientists have been obliged to look for signs of volcanic activity on the submerged slopes, also by using equipment installed on oceanographic boats.
The results have allowed the discovery of underwater gas emanation even on those islands like Filicudi, Alicudi and Salina, where signs of gas emanation don't exist on land.
Gas emissions in front of Panarea are both suggestive and impressive: some of them have a flow of more than 200000 litres a day of gas, composed essentially of a mixture of carbon dioxide, sulphur, methane and hydrogen and they are surrounded by enormous deposits of white sulphur.
The information supplied by fluid samples from the islands allows a glimpse of the existence of a still active thermic supply and with rather high temperatures. On the islands of Salina, Filicudi and Alicudi the presence of cooling magma residues seems more probable.
The research surrounding these gas emanations is still underway and is leading us to the discovery of a hidden world, which still has many secrets to reveal.

Franco Italiano

The smallest of the Eolian islands but unique in charm and beauty. Every time a ferry or hydrofoil arrives at the jetty in the little port of San Pietro, a ritual is repeated. Hundreds of people, visitors and inhabitants, are there to see who is arriving or leaving. You seem to know everybody, also because you meet them several times a day on the roads of the island, on foot (cars are banned) or on "moto-ape", used to transport luggage.
The island has a good level of tourism; in the last 30 years tourists have also bought land from the inhabitants and restored old buildings very carefully, but indiscriminately. The Eolian style was characterised by simple design, and the use of cheap materials found locally.
The typical white colour is relatively recent: in fact, the walls were left unplastered, both to save money and as camouflage against the pirates who infested these waters. One of the districts has the name of the **pirate Draugh**, who used to moor his ships there.
Panarea owes its name to the physical characteristics of the terrain **Panaria** (unconnected) - which, however, offers pleasant walks among hibiscus, caper bushes and bougainvillea, with views of the islets: Basiluzzo, Dattilo, Bottaro, Lisca Bianca, Lisca Nera, le Formiche, i Panarelli and, in the distance, Stromboli.
In the past it was called **Euonymous**, "the one on the left", in other words, on the left of ships which went from Lipari to Sicily (Strabone).

WALKS

Above the port is the hamlet of **San Pietro**, a myriad of white houses, in a semi-circle, in a multi-coloured natural setting. Climbing up on the left southwards, a track leads to the prehistoric village of **Cala Junco** in 30 minutes.
The track winds up among the houses, passing the new church of San Pietro with its lovely mosaic and terrace with a good view. You turn left and, after a flat stretch, pass the houses of **Drautto**, along the bay.
In this stretch you notice the so-called "spine", large rock formations, the remains of a lava flow which reached **Capo Milazzese.** You cross the beautiful beach of Cala degli Zimmari, which we recommend for swimming, since it

Below: view of the sea of Panarea

Opposite page: Dattilo

can be reached without a boat. From here a path with steps takes you to the promontory of **Capo Milazzese**. On the right is **Cala Junco**, maybe the most beautiful cove of the whole archipelago. A natural pool of crystal clear water with changing colours: green, blue and turquoise. You can take a dive into the blue surrounded by high basalt cliff walls, lava prisms which look like sculptures, a pebble beach and the Scoglio Bastimento and other rocks, which only just show above the surface (be careful in boats).
You must also stop to visit the **prehistoric village**. 23 oval stone huts from the Bronze Age (1400 BC) have been found. One of these, in a square shape, was perhaps the place of meeting and worship for the community. Archaeologists have found pottery, mortars, grindstones, pans and crockery, as if the people had been attacked suddenly and everything left as it was. In any case, the place they chose was perfect: a strong natural fortress. A long rock sticking out into the sea, with sheer sides, with a view which cannot be equalled anywhere.
An alternative walk, of about an hour, takes you from the

Left: Church of San Pietro

Below: mosaics from the Church of San Pietro

Opposite page: archeological digs at Punta Milazzese

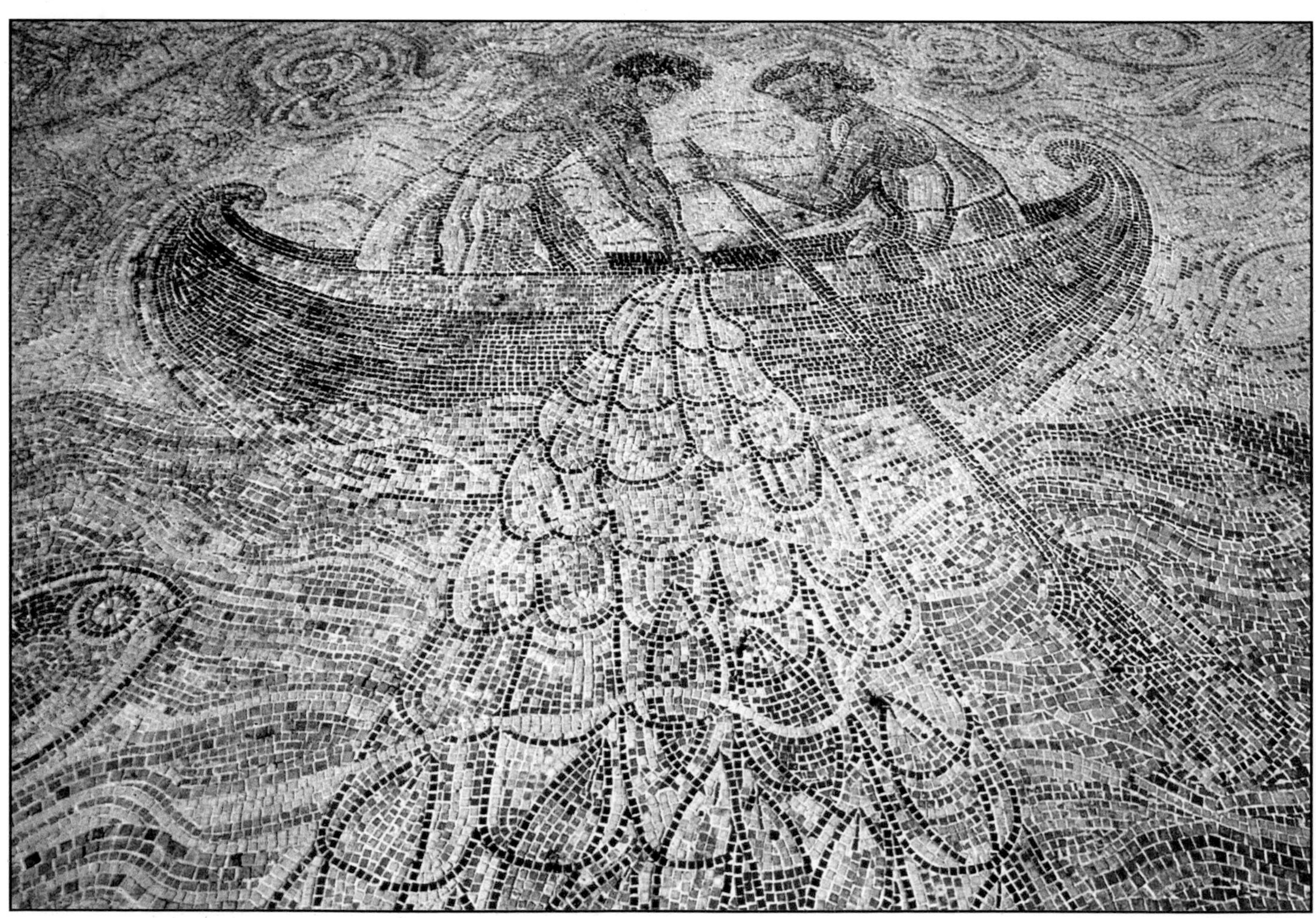

port, climbing up, to the right towards **Iditella** and **Calcara** as far as **Punta del Corvo** at a height of 421 metres. At first the track winds among white houses, shops, bars (we recommend the *granite* at the bar Naïf), and little restaurants, then it climbs sharply near the old church of Assunta ad Iditella. Further on, on the right, two houses after the grocer's **Gianni**, it is worth asking to go in and admire the view of the port and islets from a terrace set between two rocks. You continue down and, going to the right, you see the **Scoglio Sinazzola** and the **island of Basiluzzo**.
You pass Felice's house which has excellent malmsey and a small patio to sit and taste it. On the left, after the trattoria **Paolino**, the houses are further apart and the path follows a white wall, as far as the junction where, to the right, you can reach **Calcara**, a pebble beach with small fumaroles. The plateau, covered with small pebbles, was probably a place of worship until the Bronze Age. Climbing back up the road, to the right, you reach **Piana Palisi** and then the area used as a tip. From the path, at a height of 380m, you have a good view of **Punta Scritta** and the **Scoglio Pietro La Nave.** Finally you reach the highest peak, **Punta del Corvo,** from which you can observe the two sides of the island.

DISCOVERING THE SEA

You can take any kind of boat and set off to discover this charmed sea. Every day at the port of **San Pietro**, Mimmo in his cowboy hat, Bartolo Basile "il Bandito", Felicino, Saverio Cafarella and Roberto Tesoriero with his motor-sailer, wait to rent out their boats and take you to **Lisca Bianca, Basiluzzo, Cala Junco** or to sail round the island.
Your attention is immediately drawn to the small archipelago of islets and crags near the port. Not forgetting your diving gear, you set off towards **Lisca Bianca** and its lovely beach which is white like the rocks due to the fumaroles, sulphurous bubbles which have been active for thousands of years.
The fumaroles are also visible underwater, both at the western point, at a depth of 5 metres, and in the area between **Dattilo, Bottaro** and **Lisca Bianca**, 20 metres down, with hundreds of columns of bubbles. This is the crater of the last volcanic activity.
The island of Panarea, the islets, and the shallow sea which

Opposite page: top - village of San Pietro

Bottom - stretch of coastline

Below: port and village of San Pietro

surrounds it are all that remain of great volcanic activity, characterised by numerous craters now almost all submerged. This underwater platform has a maximum depth of 50 metres, so it is very accessible and the water is crystal clear. For underwater excursions you can contact the instructor **Adam Butler**, who organises courses and guided tours. For refilling tanks and diving **Roberto Buzzelli** (tel. 0330/589934). Dattilo has a pyramid form and in its sides there are some caves with crystalised sulphur and alum. **Le Guglie** are the slender crags next to it.

The island of **Basiluzzo** and the crag **Spinazzola** are full of surprises and worth a day trip. The island is 3.5 km from Panarea and has the shape of a cupola with sheer sides. You will notice the stratifications of the various lava flows, some light and other, older dark ones formed of obsidian. The rocks have very strange forms and the coast is inaccessible. There is only one landing place, near the eastern point, from which a path leads up to the peak, at a height of 165 metres (pay attention during the climb and wear sensible shoes). There is a view of Panarea and Stromboli.

The remains of a Roman villa, with traces of a mosaic floor, coloured plaster, an underground construction and a Roman dock, now 7 metres underwater, show that, even two thousand years ago, it was the residence of a "billionaire in sesterces". Today the island is uninhabited but for centuries the three hectares were cultivated. At Spinazzola, an inaccessible crag, there is a colony of dwarf palms, unique in Europe.

A sail round the island, in an anti-clockwise direction, lets you see the western side, otherwise not accessible on foot, after you have passed the quay of **Iditella** and the beach of **Calcara**.

Continuing, you meet **Punta Palisi,** the **Grotta del Tabacco** and finally a great sheer wall with the nearby crag **Pietra La Nave,** a diver's paradise: the remains of an ancient crater.

You pass **Punta Scritta**, where there are said to be inscriptions made by Saracen pirates. From here on the cliffs are sheer with basalt prisms and lava flows. At **Punta Muzza** there is the majestic cliff of **Costa del Capraio**, which drops into the sea. Then you arrive at the wonderful **Cala Junco**, the **Cala del Morto** and the **Caletta degli Zimmari**, always crowded in August, the inlet of **Drautto, Punta Torrione, Punta Peppemaria** and back to the port of **San Pietro.**

SHOPPING

If you have a little time for shopping, the boutique **Raya** will amaze you with its coloured materials, pareos from Indo-

nesia, craftware and antiques; **Cocci e Cenci** with quality pottery, **Giulio Contarini**, at the port, for Sicilian craftware, **Pucci** for patterned materials, **Gianni Spanò** with supplies of capers, malmsey and olives.

• DA PINA - A beautiful terrace with pergola and after 30 years of activity, many original recipes: fish "all'acqua pazza", fresh pasta with aubergines and special sauces, gnocchi with aubergines.

WHAT TO EAT

At dinner time the visitors dress and head for their reserved tables. The traditional place for aperitifs is the **Bar del Porto**.

Top left: Bastimento crag opposite Calajunco

Top right: shipwreck near Lisca Bianca

Below: Basiluzzo with Stromboli in the background, seen from Panarea

• DA ANTONIO IL MACELLAIO - An Argentinian offers the best T-bone steaks you can find with cooked and raw vegetables. Roulades and the famous Argentinian "asado".

• RAYA - Raw swordfish with fresh tomato, "ricciola al cartoccio" and a lovely view.

• O PALMO -Swordfish and Eolian salads.

• DA PAOLINO - A good small restaurant near Calcara: aubergines "alla Paolino" and fresh fish.

• DA TINDARO - Candlelit dinner with spaghetti and sardines, swordfish "all'eoliana" and Sicilian cannoli (hot chocolate croissants at breakfast).

• LA SPIAGGETTA - At Cala degli Zimmari: spaghetti "al nero di seppia" and with sardines. Grilled swordfish, snacks at lunchtime.

• LA SIRENA - At Drautto: fish caught by the owner.

• CURISITATI - With the backdrop of the islets, stuffed squid and maccheroni "alla siciliana".

• HYCESIA - Farfalle "alla Hycesia", fresh fish.

• ADELINA - At the port: fresh fish caught by the owner Giovanni.

• DE FRANCESCO - At the port: parmigiana eoliana and spaghetti "alla disgraziata" with tomatoes, olives, capers, peppers, tuna and ricotta.

• MOTO VELIERO PANARIA - Spaghetti "alla Roberto", Eolian salads.

After dinner try going to **Carola**, at the port, before deciding how to spend the night.

Live music and tequila. you will be in good company; you can hardly move for the crowds and it is an excellent meeting place.

Above: typical island houses

The discos **Raya** and **Cincotta** are open-air and you dance on terraces overlooking the sea.

A moonlight swim or squid fishing are good alternatives.

WHERE TO STAY

For those who would like to sleep a little after having walked, climbed Basiluzzo, swum and danced till late we recommend the so called "case dei pescatori", maybe a bit expensive and spartan, which show the spirit of the island. Just ask or follow the signs.

For those who want to book ahead:

- CINCOTTA ♥♥♥: Eolian style hotel with swimming-pool and beautiful panoramic terrace (tel. 983014).
- LA PIAZZA ♥♥♥: Surrounded by green, 25 rooms furnished in Eolian style (tel. 983154).
- RAYA ♥♥: Furnished with taste, the rooms have marvellous views (tel. 983154).
- LISCA BIANCA ♥♥: Comfortable, with rooms overlooking the port, excellent (tel. 983004).
- TESORIERO* ♥♥: Very near the port (tel. 983098).
- RESIDENCE ♥♥: (tel. 983029)
- RODA' ♥: Clean rooms and a warm welcome (tel. 983006).
- LOCANDA BOTTARI ♥: Rooms overlooking the port (tel. 983004).

Comfortable rooms to rent, at San Pietro:
from **Pina** (tel. 983030), **Tindaro** (tel. 983027), **Hycesia** (tel. 983041), **O Palmo** (tel. 983155), **Rodà** (tel. 983023), **Tesoriero Angela** (tel. 983155), **Tesoriero Giuseppe**; at Drautto: **La Sirena** (tel. 983012).

For furnished apartments, contact **Lidia Cincotta** (tel. 983197).

Below: Dattilo and Lisca Nera at sunset

TO FLEE ... TO STAY FOREVER

Two apparently contrasting themes which, when the editor asked me to express my feelings, I thought coexist in many of us. Often I've said to myself: "that's enough! Now I'm leaving." Then, after a short time, I've found countless reasons for staying. The comparison with heaven and hell immediately comes to mind. You can open the door to one or the other and you'll probably find a single world, a palette with all the colours, all the shades, all the questions and answers, or only a reflection of yourself.

Among sails coming from the north, transported by the wind, I finally realised the dream of my youth: to live on an island.

An engine breakdown and then a great love sealed my destiny,...I stayed. One foot in the sea and the other on land, I began to be fascinated by the variety of this archipelago. To the north Stromboli, with the sensation of being on an active volcano, which gives cause for reflection on questions relating to life and time; to the south Gelso, with the gentle rustling of the bunches of canes which extend across the hillside, down towards the lighthouse; to the west Alicudi, the island of sweethearts and post-hippies. History, turbulent winds and the wrinkled faces hold together this isolated world.

To the question put to me by many of my foreign friends, "which is the most beautiful of the seven islands?", I must give an answer after many years: "All of them, because each of them corresponds to a particular mood." It is not only a question of the unforgettable views of the crags, of the cones of the other islands or Etna covered with snow on the horizon; it is not only the immense blue sea in front of the house, like a garden, in which thousands of diamonds are reflected: the southern sun, the starry Mediterranean sky, the aromas of basil and of broom, the colouring of the lava and the sulphur; the traces of the cultures of these islands' inhabitants. You can find all of this elsewhere in the world, but there is something magical, inexplicable and incomprehensible that these islands possess and I believe that if this magic could be explained, they would lose much of their charm.

... I want to flee ... I want to stay.

If I were only to think of the other aspects, of relations between the people, of the spiritual loneliness, of the transport difficulties, of the uncompleted public works, of the patronage system, of the thousand big and small problems that an island community has ...

Today it lives on its natural wealth which attracts tourism, sometimes harmful, and tomorrow?

I want to stay ... I want to flee.

I flee ... I stay forever!

Alberto Santo Bevitore (Kurt Wahlen)

ISOLA di BASILUZZO

Punta Zangona
Punta Monaco Santo
Tabutello
Scoglio Spinazzola
Grotta del Carbone
Punta di Levante

ISOLA di PANAREA

Scoglio la Nave
Grotta del Tabacco
Punta Palisi
Fumarole
Sc. Palisi
Calcara
Sorgente Termale
Punta Scritta
Castello di Salvamento
Palisi
Cala Bianca
Ditella
Torricella
Punta del Corvo
Serbatoio
S. Pietro
Punta Lariano
Soldata
Punta Falcone
Punta Peppemaria
Punta Muzza
Punta Cardosi
Grotta Polomba
la Fossa
Castello
Costa del Capraio
Scoglio del Sorcio
Punta del Tribunale
Drauto
Scoglio la Loca
Punta Torrione
Piano Milazzese
Caletta dei Zimmari
Cala del Morto
le Formiche
Villaggio Preistorico
Scoglio Bastimento
Cala Junco
Punta Milazzese

Panarelli
le Guglie
Dattilo
Lisca Bianca
Bottaro
Lisca Nera

N

"A black giant" stands out imposingly against the intense blue sea. For thousands of years the volcanic cone with its "spurts", as the roars of the explosions are called, has been like a lighthouse for mariners.
For those who approach the island, as soon as darkness begins to fall, the flame of the volcano becomes visible at 15/20 minute intervals. A timorous respect is commanded by this young volcano of 100,000 years, maybe unique in the world for its three mouths in continuous explosive activity, among the highest in Europe, 2400 metres with cone and base: **"A 5-star volcano"**.
We can let you in on a secret: the many photographs you see in books of the volcano in eruption, with enormous tongues of fire, are often obtained with a particular technique. The camera is left on a tripod, with the aperture open all night, so all the lava which comes out every 15 minutes is recorded on the film.
The inhabitants have lived with the roars of frequent eruptions for at least three thousand years. The island was initially a farming colony of Lipari and lived on only at sowing and harvest time. Then around the 16th century, the first human settlement was established in contrada **San Vincenzo**, behind the church.
The development of the island is linked to the sea. Stromboli was a stop-off for those crossing the Tyrrhenian. The myth of Aeolus, who controlled the winds from here, perhaps comes from the ability of sailors from Stromboli to tell the direction and strength of winds from the smoke of the volcano.
In the 1800's the island had a fleet of 65 sailing ships in the Mediterranean, which connected Sicily with Naples. The introduction of steam ships and the opening of the railway from Naples to Reggio Calabria, sent the island economy into crisis.
To add to the difficulties there were violent eruptions and a sea-quake in 1930 with 30 metre high waves which caused most of the population to flee.
From 5,000 in the early 1900's the population has declined to 400, also because of emigration to Australia.
Then, as for Vulcano, a film rekindled public interest in Stromboli.
In 1949 the director **Roberto Rossellini** made *"Stromboli"* with **Ingrid Bergman**. In Via Vittorio Emanuele there is a plaque which shows the house where the two had their love affair.
In the last 40 years some new inhabitants have arrived from Campania and Sicily.
In summer there are numerous commercial activities thanks

to the visitors who have changed the traditional character of the community. Stromboli, for the ancients **Strongyle** (round), has two landing-places. The first, **Pertuso**, (Pertugia) is on the south-western side, in the village of **Ginostra**. Here the hydrofoil stops off-shore and a boat carries you on land. It is the smallest natural port in the world, big enough for just one boat.
The second, to the east, more convenient but less romantic, is the **Scari** (port) of the village of **San Vincenzo**. From here to **Ficogrande** and **Piscità** there is a series of beaches of pebbles and fine black sand, typical of the island.

DISCOVERING THE ISLAND

Leaving behind us the beach of Scari, with its fishing

boats and the coast road we climb up towards the **Church of San Vincenzo**. It is a narrow road, very lively in summer. The houses are not close together and you can still see some in old Eolian style: white cubic houses which stand up better to earth tremors. Architecturally simple and practical with yards and “e pulera”, circular columns which supported the trellis-work “cannizzi” used for drying grapes in the sun.
The walk is pleasant among palm trees, cacti, caper bushes, geraniums and bougainvillea. You arrive at the church of San Vincenzo and get a view of the village from its terrace. It is a small shrine of 1615 which became a church in 1725 and has been enlarged and restored. Nearby, in the sea, **Strombolicchio** stands out, a large crag which looks like a fortress. It is part of the internal and modified lava of the oldest volcano in the islands.
From the church a track leads, almost straight up, to the top of the volcano. The path climbs from 195 metres at

the **Semaforo di San Vincenzo** to 450 metres at **Prima Rina**, without difficulty: there is a beautiful contrast between green bushes and black sand.
The next part, called **Liscione**, is difficult, rocky and subject to landslides, so a guide is recommended (at San Vincenzo **Nino Zerelli**, tel. 986315 and at the port of Scari **Antonio Aquilone,** tel. 986211, **Mario Zaia**, tel. 986315 and **Salvatore Carbone**).
The reward, after two hours of climbing, is the spell of

Top: house where Ingrid Bergman stayed with Roberto Rossellini

the craters. At this point we suggest you continue to the **Pizzo** and, along a narrow path, the **Vancori**. This is the highest point of Stromboli, with a sheer drop down to **Ginostra**. From here, with good visibility, you can see Etna, Sicily, the Straits of Messina and the Calabrian coast as far as Scalea.
From the church of San Vincenzo it is also possible to head for **San Bartolo**. During the walk the houses are very scattered, but come closer together around the church, built in 1801. There are numerous paths which lead down to the shore: peaceful and worth seeing for the colours and smells of the plants and the architecture of the houses.

WHERE TO SWIM

If you haven't got a boat, there are many lovely little coves. We recommend **three black sandy beaches**: the less crowded **Forgia Vecchia**, 300 metres south of the quay at Scari, in the beautiful setting of the sandy expanses coming from the summit of the volcano down to the sea; **Ficogrande**, easy to reach, halfway between Scari and Piscità, with bars and restaurants and Strombolicchio nearby; finally the long sandy beach after **Piscità**.
From here a mule-track takes you, with three hours climbing, to the **vulcanological observatory** on the ridge opposite the **Sciara del Fuoco** and the **Pizzo** (918 metres). The craters are just 100 metres away and it is a spectacle to watch the regular explosions.

DISCOVERING THE SEA

Leaving the port of Scari we head for **Strombolicchio**, after following the long beach of Scari and Punta Lena. The crag sticks up 50 metres out of the sea and is topped by a lighthouse. It is accessible by a rusty metal stairway and then steep steps cut out of the rock. Colonies of seabirds nest everywhere. The rock, shaped like a

Colours and architecture of the island

Next page: Scari beach and San Vincenzo village

THE CLIMB TO THE CRATERS

The ascent to the craters of Stromboli takes place along a steep pathway which, from the inhabited area, leads first to Punta Labronzo and then rapidly climbs up to Pizzo sopra la Fossa (918m). It's a lovely walk in the midst of the extraordinary natural sight of the frequent volcanic explosions through which it's possible to think back over the geological history of this island, from its old base, called Paleostromboli, to the present volcano.
Coming from Sicily to the Scari quay, the southern coast of the island shows a lot of deep valleys, bordered by steep slopes made of scoriae alternated with lava streams. These are the deeply carved slopes of the old volcano which one hundred thousand years ago emerged from the water and which constitutes the frame of the island. In the northern and western area the most recent material, thrown out in the last twenty-six thousand years, has completely covered the old volcanic structure: in fact the villages of Saint Vincent and St. Bartolo and the small pathway leading to Punta Labronzo lie on the sides of the most important among the recent volcanoes, the so-called Neostromboli.
It was a very active volcano, whose flows covered the western side of Paleostromboli and now are hidden by the cane-brakes near the sea and by a thick Mediterranean bush further up. On the pathway to the Pizzo, about 600 m above sea level, it's possible to meet thin rust-coloured lava flows which represent the last obstacle a walker has to overcome to get sight of the most northern among the active volcanoes. The sensation of being on an active volcano is clear while walking along the first bends of the top pathway when below you can see the "Sciara del Fuoco", a vast hollow in which all materials thrown out from the craters are canalized. It is possible to hear simultaneously the echoes of the explosions coming from the top of the volcano and the volcanic bombs on the bottom of the Sciara. After being flung into the air, such materials fall to the ground, roll along the slope and dive into the sea very loudly.
When on top of the Pizzo, after about three hours' walk, the sight a visitor has suggests at once the sensation of being on living ground. The dense smoke, the yellowy colour of the ground and the acrid smell of sulphur give the sensation of approaching hell's door, but it is the frequent explosions that call the visitor's attention to what makes this island unique: the crateral terrace which stands 120 m above the Pizzo and which contains the three active craters with their numerous eruptive mouths. The Pizzo is what remains of the border of an ancient crater (that of Neostromboli) whose western part dropped into the sea about five thousand years ago. Its vertical walls are still visible at the sides of the "Sciara del Fuoco". In the hollow, provoked by the vast landslide, the present craters have formed, which with their erupted materials have only partially filled the old depression. This geological process is not new to Stromboli: it's enough, in fact, to have a look southwards and observe the Vancori ridge, which represents the remains of an older volcanic centre, which dropped into the sea about 13,000 years ago.

Above: eruptive mouths of the Volcano

Left: aerial view

The frequent and rather regular eruptive activity of the volcano is always accompanied by strong explosions and by the emission of bombs and lapilli that in the evening and at night becomes a firework display. Observation from the Pizzo proves captivating and the explosions show numerous variations both in intensity and typology. Sometimes they consist of jets of melted lava accompanied by acute hisses, produced by small and sharp cones which take the name of "hornitos" (small ovens in Spanish), other times of big explosions which disperse in the air a large quantity of incandescent bombs and lapilli, accompanied by loud, deafening bangs. Southward you can often observe clouds of black ash coming out of the crater which, after climbing up into the air in the form of columns, drop fine sand onto the visitors' heads, obliging them to take a dip in the sea at the end of the excursion.
This eruptive explosive activity is produced by large bubbles which flow out of the melted magma coming from the eruptive mouths. On the basis of the sizes of bubbles and of the frequency of their appearance, we can have the wide range of eruptive activities mentioned above and which together give birth to that special activity defined as "Strombolian" by vulcanologists.
This eruptive behaviour is common to all basaltic volcanoes of the Earth and represents the most frequent type of volcanic activity.
The view of this extraordinary geological phenomenon is relatively safe for visitors from the point of observation of Pizzo sopra la Fossa. Such a view may be pleasantly remembered provided you arc prudent. The bombs that accompany each explosion can reach the weight of tens of kilos and a temperature of 1000°C, and their impact with a human body might prove catastrophic. Such protections as crash helmets or heavy clothes are useless. Approaching the mouths in order to take photos or film is not advisable. We advise visitors not to go too near the small stone barriers (the so-called outposts), unconsciously erected near the southern crater, since no protection from the falling materials is guaranteed. Never descend to the narrow saddle under the Pizzo, near the active craters, because it is a dangerous area where eruptive materials often fall back and the volcanic fumes make breathing difficult.
Even if the eruptive materials fall back near the craters, it's very wise not to stay the night on top of the volcano. Stromboli, in fact, like all active volcanoes, may undergo rapid changes as far as the intensity of eruptions is concerned: they cannot be easily foreseen and can affect the whole summit area, Pizzo included. Stromboli is a mountain and as such it presents some areas with great difficulty of access, especially at night. The unevenness of the ground and the constant eruptive activity advise the help of expert guides who know the volcano well and who are aware of the conditions of the eruptive activity. They can help tourists in their excursion, showing them the natural beauty of the landscapes they see and making the view of the most longed-for spectacle, the "firework display", safe but beware of the materials falling near the craters!

Mauro Coltelli

Above: Sciara del Fuoco

Right: view of Stromboli at night

horse's head, is characteristic, but an underwater visit is really surprising. You just need mask and flippers. Strombolicchio, so rugged above the surface, is a stone column rising from the sea bed. The sides are smooth and, despite the clear water, it is impossible to see the bottom. You see red anemones, star-fish, sponges, corals and numerous colonies of orange-coloured astroides along with brown and yellow algae. It is exciting!
An underwater crag is situated just a few metres from the north face of Strombolicchio and is inhabited by many forms of sea life such as sea-pike, shiny-saddled bream, small tuna, large sea bream and large groupers. Sailing on past the inlets of **Piscità**, you meet a long black beach, **Punta Labronzo** and the **Sciara del Fuoco**, a wide black slide-shaped hollow where the debris and lava from the volcanic explosions flow between two rocky walls. It is better not to get too close to the shore. A dive is recommended. Rounding **Punta Chiappe**, you find the **Timpone del Fuoco**, on which the village of **Ginostra** stretches out. Its landing place is a hole between the rocks, which allows in only one boat at a time.

Above: Punta Lena and, in the background, Strombolicchio

Right: sea around Strombolicchio

You climb up to the village on a steep mule-track with wide stone steps, passing the yard of the **Church of San Vincenzo**, not only a place of worship but also a meeting point for the thirty inhabitants. It is an **oasis of peace** and simplicity: the white houses, almost all deserted, the silence, the dignity and pride of the inhabitants, accustomed to loneliness even for weeks at a time, when the sea is rough and Ginostra is completely isolated. Continuing the tour of the island and rounding **Punta Lazzaro**, the conical structure of the mountain is clearly visible. Gorges and rocky slopes up to **Punta Lena**, which is flat and covered with reeds. Then **Punta dell'Omo**, suitable for diving to see the rich fish life. For organised dives or equipment rental contact **Strombolania** (tel. 986390) or the **Sirenetta Diving Center** (tel. 986025). After Forgia Vecchia you are back to Scari.

AT DUSK

On all the other islands the evening is spent in conventional ways, an aperitif, dinner, the disco, but on Stromboli there are also other possibilities.
Every evening, groups of people meet up, adequately equipped, to spend the **night on the volcano**. Others board boats at Scari to go under the **Sciara del Fuoco** and watch from the sea the spectacle of incandescent rocks. When there are violent eruptions, as happened in 1985, the flow of lava slides down the slope and ends up in the sea giving off great columns of steam.
Others take part in the night's squid fishing or dine, either on a boat, or at Ginostra, and come back very late.

Top: village of Ginostra

Above: Ficogrande beach.

Right: stretches of coastline

For these night-time trips, or just to rent a boat, you can contact **Paolo Sforza** (tel. 986264), **Pippo** (tel.986135), **Stefano** (tel 986003) **Strombolania** (tel. 986115) and **Libera Navigazione Stromboli** (tel 986023).
Finally **Rinauro** (tel. 986156) for catamarans, windsurfs and canoes.

SHOPPING

This is not a fashionable island, but you can certainly find special things to buy. The boutique **Gioacchino** at Ficogrande is the best on the island. There are cool linen garments and popular pictures painted on glass by the German artist **Jurgen Werner**. Wines, almond paste and cosmetics at the **Compagnia delle Eolie**. **Gaetano Russo** for lava stone sculptures. **L'arte già nata** run by Sig.ra Elvira Pirozzi in Via Roma. **La Giara** boutique in Via Vittorio Emanuele and health products from **Pino Restuccia.** Capers, olives and malmsey from **L'erborario delle Eolie**; the **Blu Bazar**, on the main street, offers a vast assortment of local craftwork, clothes and very refined old jewellery. We also recommend Zaia for newspapers, books, cigarettes and anything else you need.

RESTAURANTS AND TRATTORIE

• DA ZURRO - near the port, terrace overlooking the sea, excellent Sicilian cuisine with Stromboli flavours. Fish hors d'oeuvres, fresh tagliatelle "al nero di seppia" with prawns, lobster and tomato. Ravioli with grouper.

• LOCANDA DEL BARBABLÙ - Cuisine from Veneto-Campania mixed with Eolian. Pasta with anchovies and mint, ravioli with aubergines, and swordfish.

• PUNTA LENA - the chef Stefano offers spaghetti "alla strombolana", fresh fish cooked in salt, paper or roasted on lava stone, scorpion fish casserole. View of Strombolicchio.

• IL CANNETO - simple but genuine cuisine, sea-food hors d'oeuvres and swordfish skewers.

• AI GECHI - a terrace with a view of the volcano and the

Above: Church of San Vincenzo at sunset

Opposite page: Piazza San Vincenzo

sea, mediterranean cuisine, fresh homemade pasta, potato gnocchi "alla bottarga", pasta with prawns.

- VILLA PETRUSA - at Piscità, genuine cuisine, maccheroni with courgettes and fish soup.
- DA LUCIANO - Trattoria, pizzeria with terrace overlooking the sea.

At Ginostra il PUNTAZZO, where the Orlando brothers prepare good fish dishes or wild rabbit.

At the observatory there is a pizzeria worth trying, if only for the setting.

La Lampara and La Trottola for pizzas and snacks; pizzas "alla romana", thin and crispy at the Pensione Roma and, finally, the Tartana Club and the Ingrid Club.

AFTER DINNER

The fashionable meeting place for an aperitif, ice-cream or glass of malmsey on the sea-front of Ficogrande is the **Tartana Club.** Also at Ficogrande is the Blu Latino Caffè. You can sip cocktails at the Locanda **Barbablù** in Via Roma. You can taste *granite* and homemade ice-cream at the bar **Ingrid** (in memory of Bergman), on the terrace near the church of San Vincenzo. The **Beach Bar** at Scari, the new bar-pizzeria **Malandrino**, near the hydrofoil jetty, with its excellent ice-creams are the meeting points of the island. For younger people, the **Tiburon**, disco-pub at San Bartolo. The disco **Splash**, behind the village, offers unbridled enjoyment till dawn.

WHERE TO STAY

- LA SCIARA RESIDENCE ♥♥♥: At Piscità, 10 hectares of parkland near "Lo Scalo dei Balordi", the "Approdi di Ulisse". Period furniture and white villas in the park. Swimming-pool and windsurfing (tel. 986121).
- LA SIRENETTA PARK HOTEL ♥♥♥: Among flowers and plants, on the black sand of Ficogrande; white Eolian architecture. Swimming-pool among the olive trees. Diving centre (tel. 986025).
- VILLAGGIO STROMBOLI ♥♥: At Ficogrande, on the lava rocks with two lovely beaches. Ex. CAI shelter (tel. 986018).
- OSSIDIANA ♥♥: Near the black beach of Scari. Open all year (tel. 986006).
- MIRAMARE♥: Beautiful views. Traditional family-run (tel. 986047).

• BARBABLU'♥: Guesthouse in the centre, small but refined, antique furniture. Comfortable (tel. 986118).

• VILLA PETRUSA♥: Rooms in a shady area near the church of San Bartolo (tel. 986045).

Other quiet and central locations:
Pensione Roma (tel. 986088) and the Locanda Stella (tel. 986020) near the church of San Vincenzo; the Locanda Brasile (tel. 986088) and the Casa del Sole near San Bartolo; the Casa Limone (tel. 986047), the Nassa sul Mare (tel.986033), Acquario (tel. 986088), Aquilone (986033). For furnished apartments: Palino (tel. 986026), Giano Residence (986141), House Service (9813169).

At Ginostra:
the Locanda Petrusa (tel.9812305) and rooms for rent from Lo Schiavo (tel. 9812880).

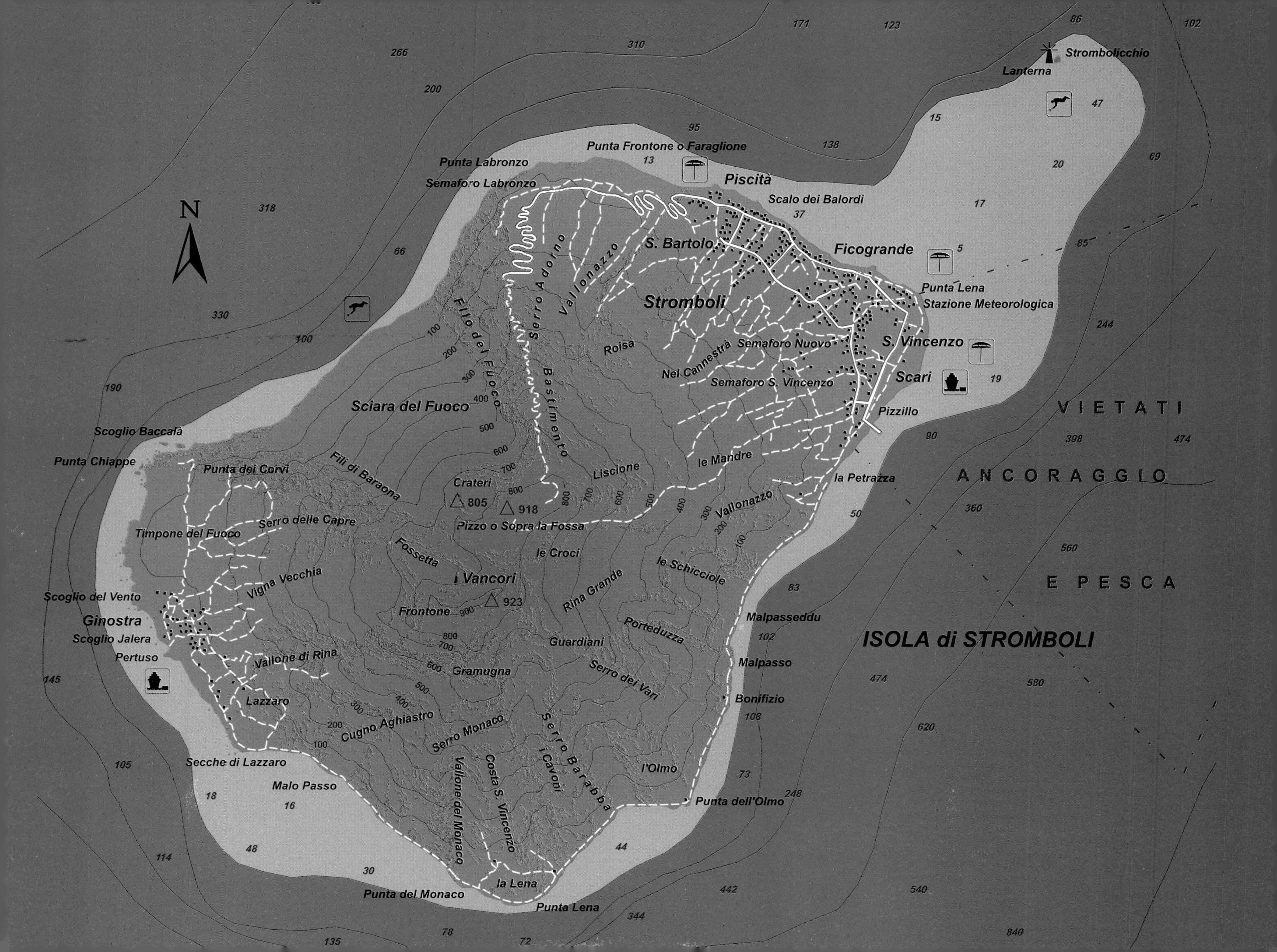
ISOLA di STROMBOLI
VIETATI ANCORAGGIO E PESCA
N
Strombolicchio
Lanterna
Punta Frontone o Faraglione
Punta Labronzo
Semaforo Labronzo
Piscità
Scalo dei Balordi
S. Bartolo
Ficogrande
Punta Lena
Stazione Meteorologica
Stromboli
S. Vincenzo
Scari
Pizzillo
Serro Adorno
Vallonazzo
Roisa
Nel Cannestrà
Semaforo Nuovo
Semaforo S. Vincenzo
Filo del Fuoco
Bastimento
Sciara del Fuoco
Scoglio Baccalà
Punta Chiappe
Punta dei Corvi
Fili di Baraona
Crateri
805
918
Liscione
le Mandre
la Petrazza
Vallonazzo
Pizzo o Sopra la Fossa
Timpone del Fuoco
Serro delle Capre
Fossetta
le Croci
i Vancori
923
le Schicciole
Scoglio del Vento
Vigna Vecchia
Frontone
Rina Grande
Ginostra
Scoglio Jalera
Pertuso
Malpasseddu
Porteduzza
Guardiani
Malpasso
Vallone di Rina
Gramugna
Serro dei Vari
Bonifizio
Lazzaro
Cugno Aghiastro
Serro Monaco
Serro Barabba
i Cavoni
Costa S. Vincenzo
Vallone del Monaco
l'Olmo
Secche di Lazzaro
Malo Passo
Punta dell'Olmo
la Lena
Punta del Monaco
Punta Lena

FILICUDI

Spring comes early to Filicudi and brings with it an explosion of multi-coloured flowers, making it a beautiful time of year to walk along the ancient pathways which cross the island.
The pathways and terraces, laid down over the centuries to allow the cultivation of the land, are a marvellous and impressive example of human endeavour.
The pathways, made of earth or stone slabs, are about a metre wide to allow the passage of donkeys, which are still necessary today to reach many parts of the island.
Capers, vines, olive trees and carob trees are characteristic of the wild countryside, dominated by red rocks with various weather-beaten shapes. Hills and valleys give the countryside a broken look.
The Mediterranean bush covers the entire island and is particularly thick on the northern side. The coastline is not sheer but gradual, creating a variety of colours in the sea from green to blue and violet.
Then there is the ***Grotta del Bue Marino****, with its mystical atmosphere, and finally* ***La Canna****, a rock about 70 metres high: a black blade sticking out of a blue sea.*
The climate, the brilliant light, the gentle violence of Mediterranean nature, the perfume of its bushes and the silence make this island almost unique.
Filicudi is still considered remote today, even by the inhabitants of Lipari. In reality, this feeling of remoteness is not a question of distance but something deeper: it is a difference of time and of the way of life of the island and its people, a remoteness from the everyday world. Filicudi is not just a place for bathing and summer holidays and, if you really want to appreciate its uniqueness, you should visit the interior, especially between the months of April and June and from September to November, when the crowds have left.
It is a wonderful feeling to walk along the pathways in complete silence, accompanied only by the wind and, at dusk, to see the many ruined houses standing out against the sky. It is striking to walk below or above the impressive terrace walls, which seem to be standing by miracle. You will be moved by the people's kindness when they greet you and they are always ready to help you in any situation.
The sky on Filicudi is marvellous, unspoilt by street lighting, making the stars stand out brightly and making it a magical experience to walk in a full moon.
The structure of the houses has remained unchanged and the multi-coloured façades create a naïve effect. Let's hope that Filicudi will remain like this, harsh and wild: that's why people come here.

Gisella and Aldo Ardizzone

Filicudi seen from Capo Graziano

La Stiva, which sells jewellery and clothing, the restaurant **Nino sul Mare**, well-known for its spaghetti with lobster and "alla filicudara" with capers, olives, anchovies and rosemary, the restaurant and take-away **Ippocampo**, a supermarket and boat and moped rental **Da Pino**, with the possibility of tank refilling and a diving school (tel. 9889984). If you want to buy fresh fish, ask for **Pino tre**, or **Samuele** with his unmistakable blue boat. The Hotel Phoenicusa ♥♥♥ (tel.9889946), to the right of the quay, is the biggest hotel with rooms overlooking the sea and a pebble beach. following the paved road, and passing Capo Graziano, you arrive at **Rocca di Ciaule**, the central point of the island. There isn't a single village, but a series of small groups of houses with different names. At Rocca di Ciaule, the hotel and restaurant **La Canna** (tel. 989956) is a typical Eolian building in a panoramic position, looking over the port and Capo Graziano. The spaghetti "alla carrettera", pasta with broad beans and the sauce made with tomatoes "a scocca", basil and paprika are all excellent. Ask Signor Pietro to let you taste his **malmsey** and the fruit from his garden. The guest house Villa La Rosa (tel. 9889965) known as **Da Lucia**, is a restaurant, bar, grocer's, baker's, pizzeria and even a disco: it is the meeting point of the island, both for tourists in the summer and

The island of Filicudi has two landing-places, **Filicudi Porto** and **Pecorini Mare**. The latter is currently not used by ferries and hydrofoils, due to unfinished work.
You will, therefore, arrive at Filicudi Porto, an attractive wide cove, dominated on the left (as you arrive) by **Capo Graziano**.
A path takes you, in fifteen minutes, to the summit of **Capo Graziano**, a natural fortress, where the remains of a **prehistoric village** are visible. The site is fenced off and to visit it, you must enquire of the custodian at the port. The stone bases of the huts and the valuable pottery found there, and now on show in the museum of Lipari, bear witness to the importance of the island since the **Bronze Age**. Capo Graziano gave its name to the Eolian culture of that period. Moreover, near **Piano del Porto**, a more ancient settlement has been found.
Filicudi Porto is quite lively in summer and here you can find most of the services the island offers; the ferry and hydrofoil ticket offices, the only tobacconist's, the chemist's and the shop

This page: archaeological digs at Capo Graziano
Opposite page: top - Filicudi port
Bottom - Capo Graziano

Siremar

the locals in winter. The specialities are: maccheroni with wild fennel and swordfish skewers with lemon leaves. Stefano will make you feel at home with his generosity and courtesy.
Il Boschetto, restaurant and pizzeria, is cool and shaded, particularly pleasant in the evening, serving barbecued fish, homemade pasta and "saltimbocca alla filicudara". From **Rocca di Ciaule**, the road continues to the right towards **Lisco Valdichiesa** and **Portella,** where it ends in a little square. In this corner of Filicudi, overlooking the sea with lovely views, you are assured of coolness and peace, even at the height of August. To the left it passes through **Canale**, **Pecorini Alto**, **Stimpagnato** and finally, after a steep downhill stretch, reaches **Pecorini Mare**, which some humorists have defined as "the fashionable place for unfashionable people".
In the little square of this fishing hamlet there is the guest house and restaurant **La Sirena** (tel. 9889997) famous for its swordfish roulades, grouper with green pepper, spaghetti with almonds or with ragù and orange. There is also the nautical centre **A.Y. Club Filicudi** (tel. 9889006) for ecological sports.
In this hamlet you can also find **I Delfini** for boat and moped rental, the shop **Lino** with its pottery, coloured pareos, wooden sculptures and "a little of everything" and the shop **Daniela** with its handmade knitwear.
If you are interested in underwater fishing, ask for Nino.
Don't miss the **Saloon** of **Zio Nino Triolo**, for all the local gossip.
Finally, at the end of the promenade, there is the restaurant **Invidia** for spaghetti "allo scoglio" and fresh fish.

WALKS

As well as the paved road, ths island is criss-crossed by numerous ancient pathways, though not all of them are easy to follow nowadays. Here we suggest some simple and interesting itineraries.

FROM ROCCA DI CIAULE TO VALDICHIESA

The walk begins in the little square at **Rocca di Ciaule**, preferably in the early morning, or at dusk. Next to "Villa la Rosa" there is a chapel dedicated to **Saint Stephen** and, to the right, a small road which takes you to **Valdichiesa** in 20 minutes. You proceed along a path which climbs up among mastic trees, brooms, thorn apples and olive trees, with a sea view. At the first junction turn left and, at the second, right and you arrive at Valdichiesa. Here your attention is drawn by the **Church of Saint Stephen**, with its particular bell-tower which, years ago, was moved by an earth tremor.
From **Valdichiesa** you can take a charming and easy walk to the abandoned village of **Zucco Grande**. Fol-

lowing the paved road towards **Rocca di Ciaule**, at the third bend, to the left, a wide track leads to **Serro**, where some caves have been turned into dwellings.

Follow the road on the right hand side of the valley, moving then over to the left. Continuing straight on, halfway up the hillside, after 30/40 minutes of pleasant walking, the steep village of **Zucco Grande**, appears. It once housed 300 people. Almost all the houses have collapsed and been buried under the vegetation, trees grow in the houses and hold up the shaky walls. There is absolute silence, broken only by the croaking of crows which slowly glide on the currents of air. A path leads to the only water source of the island, the “fontanedda” or better the trickle, given the poor flow of water.

Opposite page: village of Pecorini Alto

Above: Church of S. Stefano Valdichiesa

Right: cave used as a dwelling at Serro

SPECTACULAR SEA EXCURSIONS

On the beaches of Filicudi there is no sand but only rounded pebbles. The most fashionable is **Le Punte**; it can by reached on foot from the jetty. Alternatively, there are the beaches of **Pecorini Mare** or the **beach of the port.** Around the island there is no lack of quiet and attractive spots, which can only be reached by sea. So let's take a **sail around the island.**
From Filicudi Porto you head towards the promontory of Capo Graziano. You will notice an obvious white paint mark on the cliffs which indicates the limit, beyond which diving is not permitted, because of the **underwater archeological zone**. In the sea nearby, because of a bank 400 metres to the East, there have been numerous shipwrecks and the remains of the loads of some ships lie on the bottom. After rounding **Capo Graziano**, you pass the beach delle Punte and, further on, you can't help noticing the column-shaped rocks called **Filo di Lorami**. Then you reach **Pecorini Mare,** a fishing hamlet. Having arrived at **Punta Stimpagnato**, it is a good moment to dive into the green water of the **Groticelle** ... a great place to swim! After the imposing **Costa dello Sciarato**, a surprising stretch of coastline begins.
The **Grotta del Bue Marino** is called this by old fishermen perhaps because seals once lived there. There is no longer any trace of it but there are wonderful effects of

light and a sense of mysticism, which you feel when penetrating inside. The cave is 30 metres wide with a vault of 20 metres. The sea, over time has formed a lovely beach on the bottom and the width and depth allow boats to enter.
A few metres further on there is Punta Perciato, a lava promontory in which the sea has made an opening. After rounding the **Perciatu**, you can stop on the beach, before moving on to the spectacular cliffs nearby: **La Canna**, a basalt crag surrounded by crystal clear water (a dive is recommended to see the variety of fish) and **Montenassari** with its ridges.
The western side is inaccessible, steep and covered with brooms and ferns. You follow the coast again meeting the **Scoglio della Fortuna** and the small inlets and dovetails of **Punta Zotta** with its lighthouse. After the **Scoglio Giafante**, which resembles a tower, the countryside is wild, interrupted only by a few ancient terraces, now abandoned, and by a few houses dotted around near **Punta dello Zucco Grande** and after the Valle della Fossa and the high sides of **Monte Guardia**, you come back to Filicudi Porto.

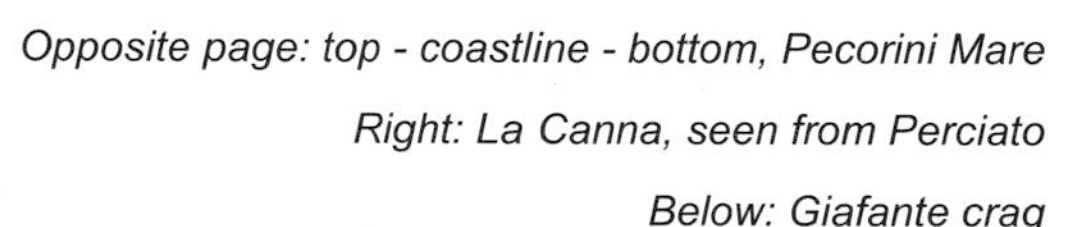

Opposite page: top - coastline - bottom, Pecorini Mare

Right: La Canna, seen from Perciato

Below: Giafante crag

THE EOLIAN ISLANDS AND ATLANTIS

Over and above their geographical position, which finds them at the heart of the lower Tyrrheanian sea, the Eolian islands "exist" essentially in a mythological sense. For the ancients, certainly, the mere fact that "pieces of heavy cliffs," against every law of nature, could float on water was proof enough of divine intervention.
This concept would explain why the Gods had stopped to rest on these islands, turning them into a permanent abode.
Just think of Aeolus, Mars, Diana the hunter and Neptune. Gods who savour here the mixture of natural elements: fire, air and water. In the same way they were fertile ground for humans: essential ingredients for magic. Historians, poets, navigators and dreamers have all had something to say about the Eolian islands. These timeless narrators were clearly aware that the Eolian islands were, and are, a synthesis of the collective unconscious. An unconscious which aims at immortality, as the Gods and history are immortal.
Setting aside Ulysses who, for the "eyes" of Homer, had to pass through these islands to "regain his self" abandoned at Ithaca; setting aside Circe, vestal virgin of Filicudi, where women, apart from possessing the gift of ubiquity, make a pact with the moon to determine the sex of an unborn baby, mythology in the Eolian islands is also about Atlantis. That architectural splendour disappeared suddenly and, almost certainly, because of an unimaginable catastrophe. In this case, however, Atlantis the home of oblivion, could represent a collective ancestral projection: so far nobody has managed to document its existence except in a very incomplete way.
Yet studies carried out only a few years ago by a Russian researcher hypothesise that, if Atlantis exists, it disappeared into the sea following volcanic explosions in the Eolian islands.
In a triangle, at the base of a platform of seventy square kilometres between Lipari, Salina and Panarea, there seem to be the remains of that cataclysm. A fanciful theory? It's possible! And it is also beyond doubt that a continent, even a tiny one like Atlantis, which was swallowed up from one day to the next, must have disappeared where "the earth trembles broken by its inflamed depths then returned to the abyss of salty rain...".
We are in the Eolian islands.

Luigi Barrica

ISOLA di FILICUDI

VIETATI
ANCORAGGIO
E PESCA

N

Punta la Zotta
Scoglio Giafante
Filo del Banco
Scoglio Cacato
C. Picarisi
Cordonello
La Canna
Scoglio di Montenassari
Scoglietto
Scoglio la Mitra
Scoglio Notaro
Valle Vanniranna
Punta Ariella
Faraglione
Valle la Fossa
Valle Fontana
C. dello Zucco Grande
Punta dello Zucco Grande
Siccagni
Valle Ghianda
Fossa Felci
773
Valle Corvi
Valle Collerestacci
Scoglio della Fortuna
Punta Perciato
Grotta del Bue Marino
Scoglio Cuddura
Sciara
Valle Lepperasso
Beneficio
Riberosse
Punta Lazzaro
Chiumento
Brigantini
Serro
Valle Palmieri
Monte Sardo
Valle la Fossa
Chiesa
Monte Terrione
Liscio
Fili di Sciacca
Monte Montagnola
349
Portella
Rocca
Pecorini
Canale di Ciauli
Monte Guardia
Filicudi Porto
Costa dello Sciarato
Stimpagnato
Punta Stimpagnato
Pecorini a Mare
Filo di Lorani
Piano del Porto
Capo Graziano
173
Le Punte

200 192 290 83 39 6 174 18 33 107 156 70 99 54 19 12 31 36 278 102 52 456 98 39 438 14 282 109 78 22 248 90 74 63 468 2,5 484 298 70 250

Off the main shipping routes, with few inhabitants, and untouched by the mass tourism experienced by the other islands, Alicudi still retains its natural charm. When you arrive on Alicudi, you experience a way of life long forgotten elsewhere. Here, not even the large groupers are distrustful and let you observe them freely.
Given the peculiar terrain, there are no roads or carriageable tracks at all and, consequently, no cars, motorbikes or bicycles either. In order to face the lava stairways, which are to be found everywhere, you have to rely on your own feet or the **pretty donkeys,** which are bred on the island and carry goods and luggage from the port to the houses dotted across the hillside. There are no discos, pizzerias, take-aways, pubs, shops, hairdressers' or amusement arcades, only a hotel with a bar and restaurant, two grocery stores and a newsagent's and souvenir shop; however, it is a charming place, where you can hide away and enjoy a different kind of holiday.
The ancient name of Alicudi is **Ericusa,** which comes from "erica" (heather), a plant still to be found flourishing on the hillsides and in the inaccessible valleys of the now extinct volcano. The base of the volcano is situated at 1,500 metres below sea level and it reaches a height of 675 metres on **Monte Filo dell' Arpa.**
The island is the most westerly of the Eolian islands and the first that you reach, when sailing from Palermo or Ustica. For this reason, despite being harsh and isolated and completely lacking in sheltered coves and anchorages, it was an important staging-post for mariners in ancient times.
Inhabited since prehistoric times and in the Hellenistic period, it preserves a reminder of the past in the remains of an early bronze age settlement (16th and 17th centuries BC.), which was laid out near the **Palumba** cliff. On the east coast of the island, scattered fragments of Roman pottery are to be found, perhaps the remains of some shipwreck.
Alicudi, like the other islands, suffered centuries of pirate incursions, with raids on both what little the poor inhabitants had and the people themselves, who were sold as slaves. The terror of these "visits" forced the inhabitants to flee and left Alicudi almost uninhabited for the whole of the Middle Ages, until 1600. Bearing witness to these tragedies is the **timpune delle femmine,** the name given to a rugged and difficult to reach zone, where the women and children hid during the incursions by marauders and privateers.
Repopulation, from 1600 onwards, brought a very small number of patronymics to the island, so, as a consequence of intermarrying, it has become very difficult to distin-

guish the origin of each individual.
Hence the practice of the so-called **insults,** nicknames which allow the identification of each family in the multitude of Tarantos, Russos and few others: family surnames such as "cavaddi" (horses, from the height of one of their ancestors), "mustazzoni" (from the moustache of a great-grandfather), "iatti" (cats), "friscaleddu" (the whistler) are a few of the nicknames, which give a touch of colour to the local way of speaking.
The population, which is currently under 150, was over 1,200 at the beginning of the century, before the large scale **emigration** to America and Australia. They exploited the land to such an extent that they managed to export part of the olive oil and caper production. Impressive terracing with dry-stone walls and a network of mule tracks continue to bear witness to the activity and organisation of this essentially farming community, whose principal settlements were high up, near the cultivated areas.
As on the other islands, the principal obstacle to agricultural development was constituted by the lack of water sources. The problem of water, which is exclusively rainwater, was solved thanks to a very elaborate system of water collection in tanks: every house still has its own, often more than one. Some can be found, here and there, in the fields and were fed by the few streams that formed during the rains.
The inhabitants, called **arcudari,** are well known for their physical strength, gentle giants devoted to fishing and farming, which they have now rather neglected, as shown by the overgrown terraces, in order to dedicate their time to the growing number of tourists who choose to visit this isolated place.

EXCURSIONS ON LAND

There is no road that follows the coastline of the island, so it is not possible to make a tour by land. There is only a narrow path which leads from the port to **piana della Bazzina** and, in the other direction, towards the **Palumba** cliff, near the **Pirciatu,** an arch-shaped rock which stands on the beach, in front of the Ericusa hotel.
The roads are mule tracks, with wide stone stairways, which lead to the summit of the island, **Piano Filo dell'Arpa.**
The vegetation and the disuse of the old pathways make it difficult to find your way around the network of tracks. It is therefore advisable to call sig. **Peppino Taranto** (tel. 9889902) to find a guide.
To reach the crater you should allow for two to three hours of climbing and equip yourself with comfortable shoes, in order to walk, without too much difficulty on the slabs of stone, called "i princhi", which form the pathway.
From the port a narrow paved path climbs up, passing some houses, to an old quay called scoglio Palomba. This picturesque hamlet of white houses climbs, terrace upon terrace, up the steep slopes of the volcano, surrounded by heather, reeds, prickly pears, caper and bougainvillaea bushes.
After passing the **chiesa del Carmine** and **Piano Fucile,** turn right at the first junction and, after a series of panoramic bends and a flat stretch, the mule track reaches a height of 400 metres and the **chiesa di San Bartolo,** the only important monument, rebuilt in 1821, upon the re-

Opposite page: Perciato with Filicudi in the background

Right: Alicudi beach with donkeys

Next page: view of Alicudi port and village

mains of the 17th-century sacristy. At the rear there is a large rainwater collection tank.
A little further on, having left the main path and turning left, you climb up alongside the terraces on a grandiose stairway, which reaches a plateau at a height of 500 metres. On this plateau, the remains of a collapsed crater, you find the village of **Montagna,** now abandoned and in ruins, an ancient settlement built high up for better defence against privateers.
From the high plateau you can climb up to **Fossa Gebbia** and, at a height of 662 metres, **Piano Filo dell' Arpa,** an ancient crater, now the highest point of the volcano. From here, there is a truly wonderful view.
A less demanding excursion can be made climbing from the port towards the Chiesa del Carmine. Passing through Piano Fucile, you continue towards **contrada Mulino** along an almost flat track overlooking the port, which leads to **Tonna.** This is a picturesque group of houses, huddled in the shelter of a valley and still inhabited, from which you can walk back down to the port.
A unique feature is the presence of "rifriscaturi" or **cold soffiones** which come out of underground cavities and are not hot like those on Vulcano. In older times they were used by the inhabitants as natural refrigerators for conserving foodstuffs and cooling drinks.

DISCOVERING THE SEA

A trip round the island can be made renting a boat from one of the fishermen in the port. Leaving in an anticlockwise direction, from the quay of **Palomba,** you follow the beach of Alicudi port. The coast line is almost entirely sheer drops into the sea without any significant bays or points, and only a few sunny beaches. From the sea you get an overall view: the village, the unkempt terraces, the chiesa di San Bartolo high up and contrada **Bazzina,** where the coast is a little more gentle. At this point the sea is only 5-10 metres deep and is suitable for diving, but it drops sharply to greater depths.
Further on, after **Punta Rossa,** towards the western side of the island, you can see a series of thin lava columns, called **Fili,** which often intersect from the top down to the sea, and a whole sequence of volcanic rocks and great ravines of crumbled lava debris, called **Sciare.** The western part of the island, completely uninhabited and inhospitable, is a sheer drop to the sea. Every corner has its

Below: sea around Alicudi

Right: Anthias Anthias and a colony of sea-horses

own shape and colour, never the same, and gives the impression of the dawn of time, before the appearance of life on earth.
You pass by small cliffs covered with the guano of birds, the **Sciara della Galera** (or Jalera) and the **Scoglio Galera,** rich in marine flora and fauna, with crystal clear, uncontaminated water. Here the sea bed shelves more gently and deserves a stop and a dive.
The cliff stretches out like a sword from the sea towards the coast, of which it is a continuation. Moving on you come to a very deep valley, the **Sciara dell'Arpa,** which drops down into the sea directly from the mountain top.
After punta Roccazza we find the terraces again and a small cavern with a pillar, called della Palumba, dug out by the sea. Continuing we pass by the Punta dello **Scario Vecchio** (old jetty), not a real jetty but a shelter from the northerly wind, the **Rupe del Perciato,** a natural rock arch, the Scoglio della Palomba and back again to Scalo Alicudi.

WHERE TO STAY

The hotel **Ericusa,** ♥ (tel. 9889902), near the beach, is the only hotel accommodation available, consisting of twelve Eolian houses with sea views, amongst the vegetation.
The islanders rent out houses or rooms in their own homes, just ask around or follow the signs.

WHAT TO EAT

- The **Ericusa** is also a restaurant and one of the few meeting places on the island. Its specialities include pasta "all' arcudara" - tuna, carrots, onions, basil and capers - and fish and vegetable skewers.

- **Da Silvio**, managed by one of the few fishermen on the island, offers genuine home cooking with a fish-based menu, served at one big table on a terrace alongside the sea. Specialities: spaghetti with tuna and swordfish, fish soup.

Left: Alicudi village from the sea

Below: stretch of coastline

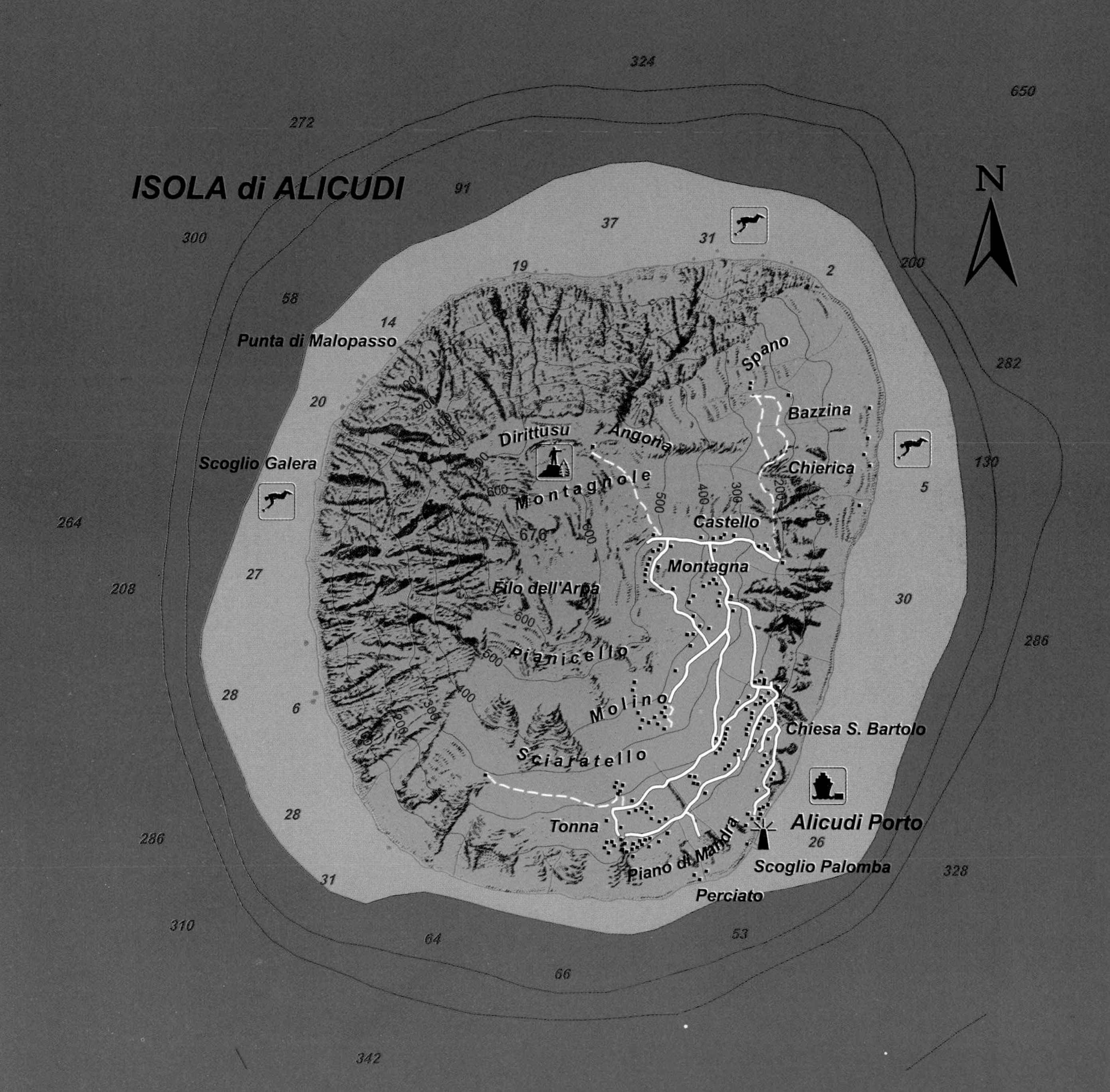
ISOLA di ALICUDI
N
Punta di Malopasso
Scoglio Galera
Dirittusu
Angona
Montagnole
Spano
Bazzina
Chierica
Castello
Montagna
Filo dell'Arpa
Pianicello
Molino
Sciaratello
Chiesa S. Bartolo
Alicudi Porto
Tonna
Piano di Mandra
Scoglio Palomba
Perciato
324
650
272
91
37
31
300
19
2
200
58
14
282
20
130
5
264
670
208
27
30
286
28
6
28
26
286
31
328
310
64
53
66
342

Contents

Maps

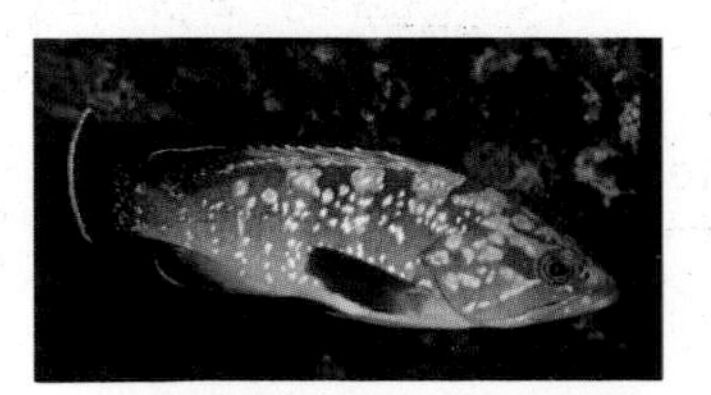

Finito di stampare nel mese di aprile 1997
dalle Arti Grafiche Italo Cernia s.r.l. - Casoria (Na)
Fotolito ***GE.SA.*** Arzano (NA)